SKELETON KEY

by

Rex Sexton

ISBN: 1544047800
ISBN 13: 9781544047805

BOOKS BY REX SEXTON

Fiction

Desert Flower
Paper Moon

* * *

Fiction And Poetry

The Time Hotel
Night Without Stars
Constant Is The Rain
Skeleton Key

* * *

Artwork, Poetry, Biographical Notes

X-Ray Eyes

Praise for *Constant is the Rain*

"Relentless pessimism about the state of the nation infuses Sexton's ... accomplished poetry and short fiction ... The title piece, about hard life and untimely death in the ghetto, introduces the book's dark atmosphere: 'Being and begetting, struggling and/ enduring ... as gunfire crackles and sirens wail/and her fate is sealed with coffin nails.' Sexton's characters – Nowhere Men as much as Everymen – are war veterans, hobos, sex workers, and blue-collar employees facing job losses ... His settings are urban wastelands. In 'The Penworn Papers' an impoverished artist recalls his degenerate life ... in 'The Gift,' a Jewish satire redolent of Shalom Auslander, a young man reverts to emptiness in his old age ... The palette is Edward Hopper's, the ironic tone O. Henry's. 'Our Town' playfully affirms Thornton Wilder's morbid vision through gloomy imagery. The poems (are) rich with alliteration, internal rhymes, assonance and puns ... They have broader application, universalizing human depravity ...Sexton's talent for social commentary and character sketching marks him as – in a title he gives a character in 'Chop Suey' – the Modigliani of the Mean Streets"

Kirkus Reviews

"Earnest and emotional, Constant is the Rain embraces desperation in tone, subject, and even in diction. A yearning for meaning in a nonsensical world comes to shape much of the text, forming the image of a people and a country existing without any defined meaning. "Sexton's poetry generally forms isolated scenes of hardship and makes up the bulk of the work. 'Like crucifixion crosses dangling weary ghosts,/the telephone poles along the lost roads of America/flash past me.' These images, producing small segments of reality, combine to show the complete picture of a fragmented people looking for solace in a world of hard truths. From the individual seeking understanding to the drug addict seeking a reprieve from existence, the characters are ... easily recognizable and empathetic figures. "Complementing Sexton's poetry is not only prose but his artwork ... most impressive about the prose ... is the continued attention to detail in diction and syntax ... the result is a work accessible to all ... that imparts a feeling that is for the people rather than simply about them."

Alex Franks
Foreward Reviews

Praise for *Paper Moon*

"Renowned surrealist painter Rex Sexton is also a highly regarded writer, imbuing his fiction and poetry with the same startling vision and mastery he displays in his artwork. His newest novel, *Paper Moon*, dazzles with words, just as his paintings do with form and color ... Sexton creates a dizzying madhouse of a world that exists beneath the surface of "normal" life. The descriptions are extremely visual ... images as vivid as dreams and often as feverish as nightmares ... the cadence so perfect sometimes that passages beg to be read out loud. Fans of Coleridge and Blake will not miss the allusions and undercurrents ... Sexton is both clever and creative, and *Paper Moon* is refreshingly intense, unusual in its complexity, and disquieting in its revelations."

Five Stars (out of five)
Cheryl Hibbard ForeWord Reviews

"Ingbar's an artist in a tough world. The sensory details — from the memories of his childhood through his imprisonment and beyond — give us to know, consistently, that the inner life carries its own salvation. If this is not adherence to "the same themes that engaged the great writers of the past," nothing is.

Julie Nichols
New Pages

"[*Paper Moon*] shows a broader picture of how stupidity and greed have made a shambles of society and the economy ... a poet and artist [Sexton] has an ear and an eye for detail, and the impressionistic descriptions help illuminate the narrative. ... Sexton proves to be an impressive wordsmith ..."

Kirkus Reviews

ABOUT THE AUTHOR

Rex Sexton (1946-2015) was a Surrealist painter, who exhibited in Chicago and Philadelphia. His award-winning art has been exhibited in museums, televised on PBS, written about in newspapers, reproduced in magazines and included in national and international exhibitions. His poetry and prose have appeared in cutting-edge literary magazines. His short story "Holy Night" received an Eric Hoffer award and was published in *Best New Writing 2007*. His poem "The Orchard" received the 2012 Annual Editor-in-Chief Award from *Möbius: The Poetry Magazine*. His poem "Ashes of Winter" was runner up for The 2011 Doctor Zylpha Mapp Robinson International Poetry Award. His poem "Gift Wrapped" was nominated for a 2013 Pushcart Prize by *Kind of a Hurricane Press*. His book of artwork, stories and poems "X-Ray Eyes" received acclaim by *Chicago Art Magazine*: "Sexton's work ... brings to mind the flattened forms and spaces and line qualities of Miro ... [and] the bizarre figures and spaces of Chagall. Bridging reality and fantasy through vaguely chimera-like figures/personified animals, and oddly flat ... pictorial spaces, Sexton's paintings emotionally engage viewers directly with multitudes of figures and multitudes of vivid expressions." He was married to the neuroscientist Dr. Rochelle S. Cohen.

FOR REX

*I lie in wait, hoping for salvation
in the memory, not of grand events,
but of those inadvertent gestures,
ordinary then, but extraordinary
now without you.*

SKELETON KEY

LIST OF FIGURES

Cover Art: Dreamers

PREFACE

This anthology is a collection of poems, stories and paintings by Rex Sexton (1946-2015). Some of the works were previously published in: *The Time Hotel, Night Without Stars, Constant is the Rain* and *X-Ray Eyes*. Others presented here are new works never published before within a collection. Rex was unable to finish the new volume on which he worked tirelessly.

Rex's art was based on his experience. He told his stories through poems, novels, short fiction, as well as surrealistic paintings. His life was governed by the creative impulse. Rex had a near-death experience when he was eighteen-years-old. This allowed him to look at life, not simply on this plane, but in deeper dimensions, questioning what we typically understand as "reality." This experience changed his life, "because [he] came back from that powerful experience altered." He seemed to have had "mystical powers: prophesy, telepathy, nothing [he] had any control over. These phenomena would overwhelm [him]." This occurrence also led to Rex's strong belief in fate. In many of his paintings, figures are represented in a doll- or puppet-like fashion. In interpreting his work, a Rabbi said of one of his works, "The Dollmaker," that, perhaps, it posits that all of us are in a certain sense extended by "divine strings," but have freedom of movement to make choices and live life fully.

And, Rex lived across the entire spectrum of life. His experiences ran the gamut of surviving poverty to discussing art, science and philosophy with the most brilliant minds of our time. He was the epitome of a person, who walked "a mile in someone's shoes." His empathy for the poor and disenfranchised was boundless and this quality is reflected in Rex's writings and art.

Rex's outlook, being fatalistic, was a dark one. Nevertheless, his love of life and its mysteries were limitless. He revered nature and the complexities of the universe, which provided optimism in a world riddled by strife. Even at the nadir of his life, he remained hopeful, as reflected in his words at the end of his last completed story: "There was lots of whiskey for Conti in his life, warm friends, loving women, starry-eyed children eager to begin. He'd love to do it again."

I arranged the poems and stories within this volume inspired by Rex's sense of hope in a bleak world. The anthology begins with Rex's poems about the promise of spring in a literal sense and in people's lives. Spring eventually fades to winter and Rex's winter poems segue into the despairing world of social injustice, war and politics. In this regard, Rex's poems are timeless, as relevant today as they were decades ago. Rex wove these themes into the act of painting and writing, as reflected in the section of poems and stories following pictures of his artwork. I end with his poems about love, some sad, others hopeful, as he was in life, and about Chicago, the city where he left his heart.

I included pictures of Rex's paintings that are among the most iconic and emblematic of his works, underscoring his strong belief in fate, his contempt for the forces that promote chaos, poverty and war, his love of nightlife and his infinite compassion for all living beings.

Rochelle S. Cohen

ACKNOWLEDGMENTS

I would like to thank the editors of the following publications in which many of Rex Sexton's poems and stories have appeared or will appear: *The Avocet, Edgz, Waterways, Hazmat Review, Clark Street Review, Möbius: The Poetry Magazine, Art Times, Nerve Cowboy, Bear Creek Haiku, Taproot, Left Curve, Back Street Review, Soul Fountain, The Pen, Write On!!, Struggle, Love's Chance, The Stray Branch, r.kv.r.y quarterly literary journal, (A Brilliant) Record, Saturday Diner, Plato's Tavern, The Rusty Truck, Fighting Chance, Lone Stars, Daily Love, Nut House, B&R Samizdat Express, Poet's Haven, Conceit, Babel, Point Mass, Children, Churches & Daddies, Napalm and Novocain, Pyrokinection, Yellow Mama, Rusty Typer, Dead Snakes, Indigo Rising, Hell Roaring Review, Wilderness Review, The Legendary, Slavia, Transcendent Visions, Caveat Lector, Poetry Corner, Marquis, Nite-Writer, Miracle,* and *Talking River.*

Passages from this work were broadcast on "The Language of Imagination" *"Talking Stick"wwwLuver.com,* Berkeley California.

An E-Book format of "Constant Is The Rain" is available through Quench Editions (www.samizdat.com/quencheditions)

I would like to acknowledge the kindness of Rex's editors, publishers and colleagues, who keep his work alive and who have given me their affectionate and kind support and friendship: Ray Forman, *Clark Street Review, Backstreet, Saturday Diner, Plato's Tavern,* Charles Portolano, *The Avocet,* Arthur Ford, *The Pen,* Debbie Berk, *The Stray Branch,*

Joseph Shields, Jerry Higgins and Elissa Yeates, *Nerve Cowboy*, Ayez Daryl Nielsen, *Bear Creek Haiku*, J. Glenn Evans, *PoetsWest*, Milton Kerr, *Love's Chance* and *Fighting Chance*, Barbara Fisher and Richard Spiegel, *Waterways in the Mainstream*, Juanita Torrence Thompson, *Mobius: The Poetry Magazine*, Malcolm Lawrence, *Tower of Babel*, Janet Kuypers, *Children, Churches and Daddies*, *Down in the Dirt*, A. J. Huffman and April Salzano, *Kind of a Hurricane* Press, Perry Terrell, *Conceit Magazine*, Richard Seltzer, *Quench Editions*, Gene McCormick, writer and artist, John W. Sexton, writer and artist, Ellaraine Lockie, poet and artist, Thomas Harney, photographer, John Brabant Lenting, artist, Jacqueline Roig, writer and artist. I would also like to thank Zoe Asta, artist, librarian and Maria Eugenia Freitas, Professor, film writer, for their affectionate friendship, inspiration and discussions. Thank you to Robert Wayner, owner and Director of the Black Walnut Gallery, artist, sculptor and woodworker, for his profound friendship, love for Rex and me and our warm conversations.

With deepest thanks to my loving and devoted sister and friend, Marion Cohen, who has always supported me unconditionally and allowed me to realize my dreams.

Rochelle S. Cohen
Editor

A skeleton key
A beggar's bones
Make up a poet's soul

REVELATION

Confined in my cloud prison,
I watch a rainbow arch across
the heavens.
Dreams shimmer through fate's prism
I crawl through life's crystal ball.

GOOD TIMES COMING

Move the sun north
the days lengthen.
Blue sky comes alive for
dreams and inspiration.
Joy on the horizon,
jubilee and revelations,
singing, dancing in the streets.
The mind spirit body is complete.
At night we'll count the stars,
catch fireflies in a jar.
The days bathed with
brilliant light. At night we sleep
under the soft moonlight.

WE DANCE SING RAVE

Life is good tonight
for a change.
Cotton clouds fill the sky
with nursery rhyme images
drifting by.
Word on the street is that the
recession finally ended.
Picture a street scene, sunny day,
blue sky, nights glitter with dreams.
Living has come alive again.
Spiraling, a gentle leaf follows
its fate along the winds
of time – greed repeats its
variables when it
can. It will be a while before
the storm comes again.

SPRING

The air is sweet, the town asleep,
I walk empty streets in the
hallowed light of a full moon
night. Above me, the stars sparkle
like gems in the heavens.
All around me a jubilee is celebrated
by the awakening crickets as they perform
their nocturnal rhapsody – to accompany
the lullaby the hushed wind whispers
through the leaves of the newly canopied
trees which line the winding lanes that
wander up and down the hills and
dales of our small town.
The days shall go on:
Full moon, new moon, Autumn, Winter,
Spring, Summer again, world without end.
Round and round the planet circles the sun,
time passes on, life moves along,
each season sings its song.
Each season brings its own wonderland.
Spring sings joy, a happy birthday to
nature after the death of winter: flowers
bloom, trees turn out leaves, birds nest,
animals birth and replenish the earth,
nature blossoms, the air is filled with the
fragrance of perfume, love is in the air
and one can't help but catch the fever.

GARDEN

Waxing moon, waning moon,
Spring melts into summer,
flowers bloom, as my garden
explodes with color, and the
air is filled with perfume.

REX SEXTON

THE SUMMER WIND

Like scrolls unrolled,
the waves unfold across
the sand and curl up again,
telling their wordless chants,
over and over, about being
and nothingness, dreaming
and forgetfulness, and the
ebb and flow of the mind
and soul.
The sea is colored by the
heavens.
The clouds are a choir.
The surf is a prayer.
The beach is a shrine to
the Divine, each comber,
like me, a worshiper
every summer.

LAST STAND

Each crashing wave falls
to make the island small,
wearing down the hills
of sand, pulling the bluffs
back into waterland.
Global warming. I
sip my rum. I understand.
Lost ships, lost dreams,
lost men.

ANOTHER DAY

Why?

I am. Do I need another reason …
does anyone … God, the Big Bang,
Revelation, Evolution?
The steps go up.
The steps go down.
The spiral staircase
goes round and round …
Wait.
Linger for a moment.
Listen to the wails of sorrow,
the laughter of children.
Imagine the journey of life
from birth to death – joy,
love, heartbreak, despair, passion,
disillusionment, longing, languor,
trial, tribulation, triumph, celebration,
loss, grief, loneliness, resignation,
regeneration, renewal, jubilation,
expectation.
Quiet thoughts, blue skies, dream …

TOUCHING NIGHT

In the rooms, between the rooms,
down the stairs, around the corners,
hallways, basement, attic, everywhere,
secrets, whispers, mysteries, in the
house I grew up in, the house you grew
up in, the world that we live in.
Full moon, my dreams tonight: people
missing, people searching …
This place I'm in, which seems to be
a playground, has walls all around.
They contain everything lost and
everything found.
Someone is hiding in a corner.
God maybe. Someday I'll look closer.
The see-saw goes up and down. The
whirl-a-twirl goes round and round.
The swings sway. The slide lets you
glide merrily down the slope on your
backside.
While the monkey bars are lit by stars,
and the future is kept in Mason jars.

ALL ABOARD

Let's go again to that enchanted land
where the mountains are highest, and
the rivers bluest, and the forests thickest,
and the grass greenest, at the top of the world
where humanity is kindest and love is
in the air and everyone is held dear.
Get a ticket from the Sandman to Dreamland
my friend. That's where the trip begins,
where it ends.

THE TIME HOTEL

It is midnight. In the dark, in bed, lying alone and naked,
I stare at the ceiling fan and smoke a cigarette. The room
is a stage set from the Twilight Zone. There is a three legged
chair beneath a wobbly table, a broken television and a one
station radio. The window won't open and its shade won't close.
The sink faucet drips, the water pipes rattle, the floor boards creak,
the radio crackles. There is no hot water in the shower in the
bathroom down the hall. There is no lighting in the hallway
except a feeble, hanging bulb. There is no paper for the toilet.
There is no lock on any door. The table lamp flickers when lighted.
The dresser drawers won't budge. It is the dog days of summer.
I hear the voice of God in the torpor, hacking and crackling through
the static of the unchangeable radio, in the heat and swelter of the
steamy Uptown night, indecipherable yet all powerful, unknowable
and unrelenting, telling me that somewhere and yesterday and tonight
and tomorrow and nowhere and always and never and forever …
There is a full moon tonight. The walls are weeping. Teardrops glisten
like diamonds in the purgatorial dark. I reach for my bottle, drink
to the hidden, like fog in a daydream, mingling shadows and moonbeams.
And moonstruck lovers sigh on their pillows.
And midnight revelers dance in the moon's glow.
And my childhood voice laughs near my window.

REX SEXTON

INDIAN SUMMER

Top down, Stormy beside me,
blonde hair tossed by the wind.
Streets of amber, scarlet, gold,
leaves flying, whirling as we
cruised along, listening to the radio
and its top ten songs.
We were free and easy that
sparkling day. Then winter came.

DARK CLOUDS

They gather in the ghettos
like preachers frozen in spirit.
Another black son has been killed
by a white policeman for no
apparent reason.
Massive arms flare, as the
like-minded brethren try to
console the younger congregants,
still a realm of graves filled
with the skeletons of slaves.
If only their lives could be
set free.
If only they could release the chains
That bind them to hatred, injustice
and bigotry.

WINTER WALK

Frozen to the bone, I bundle home across
downy drifts of mystic whiteness.
Ice angel, lifting her winter wings – all
around me in the night, as I cut through the
city's sprawling park, like icicles dangling
from the winter sky, towers rise, sleek with
glass and reflections of the nebulous.
They almost rival nature I'm thinking,
but not quite.
Strolling below, amidst the parks, gardens,
walks, fountains, of downtown Chicago, the
quaint Victorian mansions and smug old
brownstones – most of which have been
converted into pricey eateries, watering holes
and Gold Coast condos – begin to assume an
illusion of fairyland as a heavenly lake effect
snow descends on the city and flakes as big
as dove feathers (angel feathers) transform
the spires and gables into enchanted castles.
A small stone bridge over a silver stream
cascading through the darkness and disappearing
around the bend. The raw winds blow. It
all seems like a dream. The bare park trees,
like waving hands, point spectral fingers at
a falling heaven – falling on me, on all of us,
as it transforms our mundane world into an
enchanted land.

DINER

Cut-paper couples eat blue-plate specials at Formica tables –
spirits steaming from their coffee cups – in the dead of winter,
sky a shroud. *"Long ago and far away and when you wish upon
a star and ... "* Chalk white light makes ghosts of their shadows.
Apparitions crowd the counter, huddled from a grim world of ice
and rock. *"Wish I may and wish I might and once upon a time ... "*
I bundle back into the blizzard, bowed against the swirl, where
fallen angels dream of sorrow.

BIG CHILL

Night – and I think about existence
in the snowy silence.
Too bright the street lights
it seems. Dark trees tangle
even more than usual.
The road is empty, isolated.
It is a dark, bleak voice.
Tomorrow morning
will bring winter's gray haze.
Streams are frozen, pipes are
blocked. The world we
know does not exist.
This is the meaning of it all –
no meaning. Just frozen
water, stopped clocks, a
precarious balance between
life and death.
OK. Maybe it's also those
snow angels someone made
in the corner.

COLD MORNING

Shadows move through dreams
of longing. I sit with my
coffee. The park is empty.
Statues stare from and
through a time no longer there.
A storm cloud fills the air.
Crystals of ice cover the grass.
The ghosts of dead souls cross
paths with the fading pantomimes
of the latest tales that will
not last. Yet, on certain nights when
the moon is bright and the stars
light the sky, the park images
will haunt you with their
times gone by.

MISSION IMPOSSIBLE

Midnight and moonlight
shining on the snow. I sit
on a park bench all alone with
nowhere to go. All I know
is the dark side of the soul.
In the morning, dark clouds will
appear as shrouds. Church bells
will toll. Time is a thief that
binds us to blindness as the years
pass.
I'll look for a mission in the morning.
A cot and two meals – breakfast,
dinner, lights out early. All day I'll
beg change and drink life away.
I can pray. All is forgiven, your
one's sinning when that's done.
I've tried, sometimes with tears
in my eyes. Maybe a useful life
begins with that little nod to God –
or fate. But no, I'll drink all
day.
Taste my little bit of heaven
before it's too late.

SNOW MAN

No heat in my flop, I bundle up and go out
into the Hawk. That's what we call winter here,
our name for the predator. Falling snow, deadly icicles,
drifts like grave mounds, shifting with the raw winds.
Teeth chattering, old bones shivering, I trudge through
the shrouds that blanket the ground. I know a bar
that's open 'til four. It isn't far. I'll hole up
there. I'll be half passed out when they call last
round and throw me out. The cold won't matter.

REX SEXTON

THE MOX NIX BOX

Winter blows through the rattling
barracks windows and with it,
off the snow, comes the scent of
wet hair and soaked clothes, in
the memory of that rainy day we
met in a Berlin café. Pale as a ghost
you sit, I know, in your window
watching the shadows on the street
come and go, looking for me in the
only place I can't be, with you.
Mox Nix means "means nothing"
in German. I learned that during
the year I was stationed there. All
possibilities exist in a box which
remains locked. The Mox Nix Box
is filled with nothing one can use
like trinkets, souvenirs, tears.

CAROUSEL

I get up at noon, come here,
sit in my corner, drink beer,
eat lunch, scan the scratch
sheet for a score, call my bookie,
drink more, nail a winner, stay
for dinner, chat with the regulars,
all of us stuck in life's rut hoping
for some luck, work out the kinks
in my system, recording odds,
jockeys, track conditions, linger
through the evening, bolt down a
stiff one before leaving, go home,
go to bed, dream about horses,
wild, free, furious horses, like
storm clouds driven by the wind
as they race down the track
never looking back.

REX SEXTON

SILENT NIGHT

Huddled like headstones in a graveyard,
the rows of working class houses lay buried
in the blizzard – earth, air, sky all one.
We can see nothing; the world is erased.
Wind whipped shrouds swirl around.
We knock on doors, ring bells, holding
each other, searching for shelter.
STOCKS PLUMMET, BANKS FOLD,
JOBS LOST, HOUSES FORCLOSE …
Newspapers flutter around us in the
darkness; white veils whirl like ghosts.

ATONEMENT

Night, snow falling across Chicago like stardust
over tombstones. The streets are crowded with
shivering commuters who cough and shift their
glance when I stick out my hand. In the store
windows temptations sparkle. They avert their
eyes from those too. This Christmas will be poor.
The grand cathedral in the middle of the downtown
bustle. I slip inside, out of the menacing night, into
darkness adorned with candlelight, sacred statues,
flickering stained glass windows, altar, pulpit, the
son of god nailed to a cross and wearing a crown
of thorns.
In the hushed, hallowed quietude I choose a retreat
amidst rows of empty seats – a widower here, a
dowager there, another half dozen other lost souls
with their crosses to bear.
My home away from homelessness, this house of
worship, along with the soup kitchens, rescue gospel
missions, park benches, tunnels, viaducts, cardboard
boxes, shelters, bridge bases, police stations, public
libraries, museums on free days.
In the warm and mellow illusion of transcendence,
I can sit and reflect upon the mystery of birth and
death and feel a little peace and momentarily forget
my permanent state of hopelessness: roofless, jobless,
friendless. "Bless me Father for I have sinned." I say
to the man upstairs, who probably isn't there. "I cheat,
steal, connive." But not like Madoff. I brood. Not like
Wall Street. I sin to survive.

REX SEXTON

THE ASHES OF WINTER

Cold rain, winter closing in,
promising snow, icicles, and
fields adrift with mystic whiteness.
There won't be time to set things right.
There won't be time for everything.
Time dreams in a garden lush with life
blooming. Days fall like snowflakes,
melt with the spring rains.
Was there ever time ... to do anything?
You wonder.
Should you feel sadness, despair, as
you sit in your rocker and turn the last
page on the story of your life, a packed
journal bookended in black between two
eternities, all the chapters incomplete,
and soon to be erased?
But being here was never clear.
A mystery at best, all clues leading to
enigmas, paradoxes, illusive suspects,
artful dodgers that disappeared.
Shadows and dreams are all you
remember of that fire that burned bright
between those existential nights, where
you tried to do right by your family,
yourself and your fellow man.
So at this end, should you be content,
as you rock in that chair, a bundle of

regrets and tangled hair, knowing all
that remains of the ashes of winter is
the warmth you once gave?
Could you have given anything better?

REX SEXTON

STORMY WEATHER

Overcast day
your smile a sunray.

ANTHROPOMORPHIZING

They say if you stare hard enough at any critter,
monkey, dog, turtle, whatever, you'll start to see a
human face in there somewhere. Why not? They've
worn them longer.

CRESCENT MOON

shining over fallen snow.
Coyotes hunting the dark
and menacing back streets of Chicago.
They kill cats, dogs, household
pets, rabbits, squirrels,
mice and rats, deer
feeding in the woods, a derelict now
and then. A child screams every
so often.
They moved from out West long
ago looking for sources of food
more plentiful. Now fifty thousand
wild dogs dominate Chicago.

ZIGGY THE KILLER ELEPHANT

Ziggy danced in the "Follies." That's how he got his
name (Ziegfeld). He was in the movies too. A "big"
star before we were born. One day he up and killed
his trainer. They put him in our Chicago zoo. He
killed his attendant there as well and they had to chain
him in his cage. We read about him in the papers when
we were kids. It was a sad story, Ziggy's life and times.
We got to thinking about how awful it must be to be
chained up that way in a tiny cell as the papers described.
We wondered if he missed dancing. What he did all day.
We went to the zoo. We brought our harmonicas. We
figured we'd play a little music for him, cheer him up
if we could. We were all rock star musical, Elvis, Fats
Domino. That elephant was huge. He must have been
something phenomenal to take in on a theater stage. He
was so big he had no room to move. He couldn't even
turn around in any kind of way with that chain fastened
to his back leg. Ever see a trapped giant? It's hard to look
at. We started playing "up" tunes for him. "The Yellow
Rose of Texas" and so on, to get him in a happy mood.
But Ziggy just stood there, like he was deaf or brain dead
or he was too beaten down to care.
Meanwhile, all the other elephants in the house, who were
in group cells and could move about, started dancing to
beat the band. It was like a Disney cartoon. All around us
The elephants were rocking back and forth, sashaying their
hips, waving their ears. They even looked like they were
smiling and we realized that these elephants weren't out of

29

Africa or some jungle but were all castoffs from some
sideshow or circus – performing gigantos.

Then Ziggy started getting into the show. He picked up one
foot, then another, and before you knew it he was marching
in place one foot after the other, front to back, and eyeing
us as if to say: "Have I got the rhythm? This OK?"
Meanwhile, the people in the elephant house were getting
freaked. They start running in all directions, like there was
going to be a stampede – as if the caged elephants could
actually go anywhere. Some of the women screamed. So,
these security guards swoop in. We run. A secret smile on our
frozen faces as we tumble out to freedom. Ziggy still had it in him.
Ziggy still could cut a rug. It was probably the last good time
Ziggy ever had.

STRAY DOGS

... death winds howl in the black fog of
my brain as the world drops into night,
and the city and the streets and the bars
and my soul are all buried in a bottomless
night ...

We drank at the dock waiting for the truck
to haul us from Day Labor to the meat packing
plants at the edge of the Loop where, block after
block, stray dogs prowl the buildings from dawn
till dusk.

We drank as we slid through gristle and blood
shouldering sides of meat from the delivery trucks
to the slaughter rooms inside where the butchers
chopped them up, kicking off the mongrels as we
staggered in and out, who fought for the bits of meat
which spotted the grimy walks.

We nooned on Muscatel in the alley in the back.
We tossed the stray dogs lunchmeat from our
crumpled deli bags.

We drank as we swept and mopped the bloody
floors, scooping entrails into trash bags which
we piled outside the door.

As the world dropped into night, we cashed our
checks at the corner bar. We stared at our drinks
and waited for the whores.

31

OUR TOWN I

I had to get out of the city, if only for a day:
the congestion, pollution, noise, confusion.
I took a Greyhound to the nearest small town.
The Mayberry streets, lined with gingerbread
houses with white picket fences, surrounded a
lush town square with a stately, brick courthouse
in the middle of it.
I got an ice cream cone at a Baskin-Robbins
and sat outside on a bench.
The weather was perfect, sunny, warm.
A rat poked its head out of a hole in the asphalt
at the edge of the sidewalk and looked around like
a submarine periscope.
He fixed his eyes on me. I wondered if there was
some kind of recognition – that he saw that I was
as out of place as he was.
He bolted from the hole and, clutching my cone,
mouth open, I watched him walk directly to me, wary,
but resolute, moving forward on some mission.
Suddenly, he leaped into the wastebasket next to me.
I watched him dig around in the garbage and pull out
an empty malt cup. He jumped back onto the sidewalk
and gave me a final look, his teeth griping the empty
container, and then he scampered back to his hole.
He placed the upended cup beside it and dove out of site
into his underground hide-out.
His head popped up again and he pulled the malt cup over
his chambers and fixed it securely like a man-hole cover.
I guess everyone needs a quiet escape.

GLOBAL MOURNING

That moment in the night when the echoes and
apparitions of the tenement's evicted-from-life
former residents begin to haunt the tumbledown
premises, amidst the clanging of old pipes, the
creaking walls and groaning staircases, the hiss
of radiators, with their moans and spectral appearances,
is my cue to grab my coat and get my hat and hole up
in one of the neighborhood's booze and blues rattraps,
until I can numb myself from their cries and sleep
while the bedbugs bite.
I know they all need closure from their victimization
by fate and that they will never rest in peace until
they get it off their chests and attain that catharsis.
But I've heard their stories before, seen them on TV,
read about them in history: slum landlords, usury,
discrimination, exploitation, tyrants, death camps,
ethnic cleansing, aristocrats, bureaucrats, slavery,
iron fists, holocausts – every misery one can imagine
involving man's inhumanity to man. I see the sequels
of their tragic destinies all around me in the misery and
poverty I move through every day. Besides I have my
own sorry story to relate, which I'm sure I'll do when
my hard-luck lot is through and I clatter around in my
chains. You only live once. There's no second chance.
When you never got your due wailing through eternity
is all that's left for you.
I developed a theory nursing my nightly drinks in the
ghetto gin mills, surrounded by lost souls almost as
dead as the ones I fled. Tenements topple, ghettoes
crumble, civilizations fall to ruins – all of them

replaced by new habitats that will also be erased. What
do the ghosts haunt then? I think they roam the wind,
form a civilization of howling phantoms, cause
hurricanes, tidal waves, change the climate, melt the
ice caps. I believe everything they say about carbon
emissions, toxic waste, air and water pollution,
all greed and gluttony and abuse propelling us toward
the end of the world. But I think the haunts contribute
as well with their tales of living hell.

SLEEP WALKERS

Movies, dreams, life is
wished for in these but
never achieved. The rarified
dazzles the eye like clouds
floating by.

"WHAT'S IN A NAME?"

Rex Sexton, is that a pen name? People wonder. Or a nom de plume since I'm also a painter? If not, how did it come together? It does sound more than a bit designer. (A rose by any other?)

The last name's from a job title in England, I tell them, a church caretaker. My first name came from a dead boy, who had nothing to do with anyone or anything – a total stranger. He's buried on what's left of my grandfather's farm in Southern Illinois in the family plot from that time.

The small property is now owned by a cousin. The boy's family was traveling on a buckboard from Indiana to Oklahoma. This was at the turn of the twentieth century. The man had inherited some land. The boy had died shortly after birth, a blue baby, a respiratory fatality.

My grandfather gathered his family together and held a service. (The couple had happened upon his farmhouse first.) After the funeral the man had one more request. Would my grandfather name his next son Rex? Not the first name, of course, but the middle, perhaps.

It would make him and his wife feel less saddened if their son's name lived on. He would be alive in spirit, at least.

My grandfather had no problem with that. He told the grieving couple it would be an honor, that he would tend their son's grave with the same care as the others.

He had four boys already – Frank, Russell, Buck and Scott. Three girls came after that: Katherine, Elizabeth and Francis. My father was his final child. He named him Charles Rex. I first learned this story when I was forty, visiting my father. It was the first time it came up. Named after a dead boy. Perhaps it explains why I've felt haunted all my life by the meaning of life, of living and dying. I became a writer and philosopher, painter and sculptor, pondering mysteries like what happens to the souls of little dead boys traveling the lonely roads.

"HANGING TREE"

Jumble, fumble. The alarms go off. Faster than a speeding bullet the cops show up. Camacho catches the El train, rooftops interrupted by flashes of lightening. Cold, alone, pounding rain.

Full pedal, passing the bottle, Plugger races the car down the side-streets at a hundred or more. You don't ride often in a flying coffin but ain't that what life is for?

"So, he gave me inches seven," the wild white girls sing some anglo bottle of beer on the wall song variation in the back seat. "I said honey this is heaven."

Two-wheeled corner, slides, skids, the radio blasting something about things going better with Coke.

Someone say coke? Yeah man.

"So he gave me inches ten, I said double it again.

Houses a blur, whoosh, whoosh. Minds in a whirl, whoosh, whoosh.

ENCHILADAS

They flash past a curbside stand in the industrial district where their parents slave every day for minimum wage.

"Enchiladas!" The white girls giggle.

Plugger slams the breaks, slides, skids. Camacho laughs as Plugger jams it into reverse and they fishtail back.

"You no can do that." The proprietor shakes his head. "Park on the sidewalk."

They all pig out – the wild white girls with relish. They wash down the food with whiskey and malt.

"So he gave me inches twenty," the girls sing, gleefully, greasy goodness stuffed in their mouths. "I said honey that's sure plenty."

They creep cautiously down the darkened streets, through the blackened gangways, along the unlit alleys. They spotted their hit while cruising the main strip – a cluster of punks drinking beers in the bowling alley parking lot.

"Geronimo!" They whispered.

They park Plugger's junker in an alley around the corner – an old beat up taxi painted black and lettered ghostly with "Tales From The Crypt," and "Death You Deserve IT," scrawled on the sides in swirls of white – an American flag flying from the antenna.

There are a dozen of the enemy. They have to do it quickly, before the bowling alley gang gets wind of their gorilla attack and piles out on them in mass. Plugger walks straight at them, Mr. Good Wrench hidden in his army surplus jacket.

"You guys seen my brother?"

They fan out around the cars, gripping tireirons, crowbars.

"Who's this jerk?"

"It's me, Tony."

"Anyone know this punk?"

They rush them, swinging. The punks are fast. Camacho blocks a bottle. Sixteen stitches along his arm later, no problem. They beat the punks bloody. Bam, bam. No one died. The punks must have had God on their side. Next day, the punks jump them back, outside their pool hall. Have themselves a ball. Good training for war. With jobs scarce, everyone is thinking about joining up when they are old enough. Even Camacho. Why not? The streets of Iraq or here? At least you get paid for being over there. Someone has to fight the wars. Nothing in it for the sons of doctors and lawyers.

A good run. Camacho leaves the pool hall, pockets the fives, ones, puts the tens and twenties in the duty booty for his parents. Too good to leave behind, he takes his beer with him and drinks it in the alley.

Dissolving night over urban blight, the rising sun pointing at the "on the run" like a gun. All over the Dead Zone the junkies are searching the catacombs for that breakfast of champions, hidden in the labyrinths.

Being, being, nothingness.

Camacho closes his eyes and downs the beer, feels the darkness of the universe and all its shadows disappear.

"We're done man!" Skinner's teeth chatter as they sit shackled together on a lockup bench waiting for the Sergeant. "Murder one! Life man! Unless they give us death! You don't think they'll do that?"

Things happen. This one had happened fast. Camacho said "Stick 'em up" and the gun went off. They had bolted out the back door and down the alley. Camacho threw the gun in a frenzy at a backyard tree where it disappeared in the leaves.

The cops were right there. They must have been cruising by and heard the shot. Camacho watched the tree as they grabbed them, put them in cuffs, roughed them up – two troublesome looking teenagers in the middle of suspicious circumstances. It didn't fall, the gun. It must have got stuck, good, in some branch, something like a golfer's hole-in-one, or some basketball player's one-in-a-million full court shot.

"Look Skinner," Camacho whispers, "we went in the front and came out the back. No one saw us enter or exit. No one was in the old man's shop. Hey, we were just cutting through the alley. As far as they know, whoever blasted the old man went out the front while the cops were wasting their time arresting us. They got nothing except us being in the wrong place at the wrong time. Not even in it, just near it.

They got no weapon, loot, and it ain't like we got long rap sheets like hardened criminals."

"Unless the gun comes down!" Skinner hisses. "Then it's homicide!"

"Calm down Skinner. We got luck on our side. Enjoy the ride. Unless some little bird talks, we walk."

They walked alright morning, noon and night, Camacho and Skinner, alone or together in any kind of weather, up and down the alley past the tree, braced to jump the fence and snatch the evidence before it fell from some branch on the grass and the old couple who lived there found the gun and the cops had their ass.

"I'm going in there." Skinner hollered. "I'm climbing that tree and getting that fucking thing!"

"You ain't doing shit, half-wit." Camacho spat at a garbage can. They were sweating bullets. It was the dog days. Flies swarmed around them. "When the leaves fall we'll be able to spot it up there. Maybe. I'll jimmy up there faster than you can. Bim bam the monkey man. For now we leave it alone. I don't need your skinny, clumsy white ass clowning around and falling down. It's a miracle." Camacho's voice was hushed as he stared at the tree. "It's like divine intervention or something. Like God said: "Wait, fate, give them a break.""

"Miracle? It's a curse! It's torture! If you think God's protecting us you're nuts! We're killers – at least you are. If God's doing anything he's giving us a taste of hell before we go to jail!"

"So, it's just dumb luck! Don't fuck it up! You're as guilty as I am and just as damned in the eyes of God or in the eyes of The Man. Get your head together, amigo, you're going loco!"

They never even charged them at the station with anything, although they questioned them long and hard for hours. Skinner almost broke. He started crying like a baby and babbling incoherently. Luck all he bawled basically was "I didn't do it. I didn't do anything. Leave me alone." Meanwhile the pigs combed the shop, alley, backyards, rooftops,

41

and finally had to let them go when they came up with zero. Camacho had washed his hands as soon as they hit the station, jumping up and down and complaining he was about to pee in his pants. They never did that forensic gunpowder test on them anyway.

"Skinner look. It'll be OK. We'll get the gun. The shooting was an accident. We just wanted to scare the old man. We didn't want nothing like that to happen. God, fate, whatever, we got a break. Maybe a chance to change, repent, do good things not bad. Think about that. You know what they say: God works in mysterious ways."

Jesus Skinner was a handful. No cojones.

Skinner was dangerous. In his tiny, sports poster-filled bedroom, Camacho lay propped up by pillows on his bed and stared at his rumpled reflection in the dresser mirror. With his sweat-matted hair and haggard face, he already looked incarcerated. Skinner would squawk, Camacho knew, and soon. He would get some neighborhood mouthpiece. They came cheap enough. Quick and dirty plea bargains were what they were all about. He would show the cops where the gun was, testify. The miracle tree and the magically hanging gun were a gamble that Skinner's nerves couldn't handle. Could Camacho blame him? Freedom or life, all or nothing. They would try them as adults, two slum punks with nothing and no one to prop them up or hold their hand. The court would pull the chain and flush them down. But Skinner could be out before he was thirty if he played his cards right. Turn states, point the finger at Camacho. Would he do the same if it were the other way around? God, if it only had been! If only he had not been holding the gun that shot the old man.

The room was a hot box. Camacho pulled off his shirt. He tried to mop the sweat off his face, chest but the shirt was sopping wet and his efforts were useless. Through the paper-thin walls, he could hear his family talking and laughing – his mother and sisters in the kitchen cooking, his father and brothers noisily watching the baseball game in the living room. He closed his eyes and shuddered as he listened. This would kill them. His father would die inside. His mother would go crazy. His brothers and sisters would be locked up in their own little prisons with him and would sadly miss him on Christmas, birthdays, weddings, births, graduations, all the times a family came together he wouldn't be there.

For the thousandth time he reran the nightmare in his mind. It was a two-bit jewelry store, no cameras, alarms, but enough gold school rings, trinkets, wedding bands to make a take even the head hanchos in the neighborhood could celebrate. Fence it, melt it down. The price of gold was climbing through the clouds. The place was a piece of cake. He was amazed that no one had hit the store before.

But the gun went off and the old man dropped. He dropped like a rock. It wasn't like the shootings you see on TV. It was like the old man was a puppet and Camacho cut his strings.

"Julio, we gonna eat now!" His sister Maria shouted from the kitchen. He could hear the clatter of plates and utensils, the sliding of chairs. He couldn't face them.

"Pronto Julio!" His sister Nanette shouted and laughed. "You don't come quick we gonna eat it all!"

"Eat it all! Eat it all!" Little Fernando laughed and stomped around the living room floor.

Camacho rose slowly and faced his reflection in the mirror. Julio Camacho, he brooded, the pretty boy with the ugly name. Camacho meant humpback. *"We're all humpbacks in this neighborhood,"* was one of his father's favorite jokes, *"we're all bent over by the burdens of the poor."* He felt another weight on his back now. The weight of a murderer. This weight he couldn't throw off, despite all his sculpted muscles. He was a champion wrestler on the high school team, at least in his weight class, short like most Mexicans but strong and quick. If he stuck out two more years of high school and managed to pass, he could probably get a college scholarship. But that was a gamble *he* couldn't handle. Try as he might, he could never get the complexities of math or science, or that world of chemicals and gases, all those protons, electrons, neutrons, formulas, equations, astronaut stuff. Camacho felt a fool in school. The champion with his muscles was El Stupido in the classroom. This delighted his teachers who liked to stick it to him, "that cocky Camacho kid." *"Mr. Camacho, today's lesson seems to have you in a strangle hold. Maybe you should exercise your brain now and then? Instead of biceps and pec try to put some muscles in your head."* To save face he played it down, swaggered around. "Fuck that book shit!" He would blow it off to his friends. "Who needs it?" They felt the same way. Brains were a liability. Didn't that honor student in the black neighborhood just get beaten to death because he wanted to study and not join the gang? Besides, did book brains ever do anyone any good in the hood? His odds for getting out of the ghetto, like theirs, were zero. So, say he did get into college; how long would he last? So he could wrestle; was he Olympic material? The gangs were all he was good for, Camacho knew, committing crimes, running drugs. His glory days were here and now on the streets where he could flash money and strut his stuff. But that street of dreams had its dead end coming. It was written on the walls with graffiti scrawls. *"Eat, drink and be merry amigos."* Their leader Pena would salute them with his toast. *"If you don't die on the streets you'll die in jail."*

"Poppy, I got to get out of here." Six months ago, he had sat down at the kitchen table with his father after the party they had given him on his sixteenth birthday. The tiny, appliance cluttered room with its faded walls and warped linoleum was still decorated with streamers and balloons, as the rest of the house had been, courtesy of his sisters' talented hands. *"I want to join up. Next year. If you sign for me, I can start the papers now. Be a Marine. I can get my GED while I'm there. Pursue a military career."*

His father was sipping a beer. He looked tired and old beyond his years. He had spent his life in these South Side slums, before and after he had served in Desert Storm; and the mystery to Camacho was that he never seemed to regret a day of it, even though he must have seen and lived a life of hardship without let up.

"You want to go to Iraq?" His father had lifted his eyebrows. *"You want to get blown up? Do you know what war is muchacho? I don't think so. No. You finish school, get a job, wife, have a life. Of course, when you turn eighteen you can do what you want. Like I told you Camacho means hump, you want also to walk with a limp, be blind, crippled? Be my guest."*

"But it's no good here Poppy." Camacho's mind swirled with the life in the hood, drugs, guns, gangs. Things were different now then they had been for his father when he was a kid, no matter how bad things were back then. It was a different world. If you didn't join a gang now you were a marked man. *"Es muy malo aqui, Poppy."* Camacho pleaded.

"Malo? Bueno? If it's no good here," his father tapped his heart, *"it's no good anywhere."*

"Julio, we're waiting!"

"Un momento, Mama. I got to change my shirt!"

Camacho fished a tank-top from the dresser and pulled it on. He pondered his biceps, dark eyes, wavy hair. What the zombies wouldn't do to him if he landed in stir.

"I'm almost there! Presto. Change-O!"

He glanced at the window as he ran a comb through his hair. After everyone was in bed he would slip down the fire escape. He would meet Juanita in the church yard, go drinking with his friends. He had to get out of there, get some air, get high, forget about Skinner, the murder, before he lost his mind.

A peek-a-boo moon in a storm chased sky, like an avenger's eye peering through its cosmic keyhole at the sinner below, watching for the chance to transform the night into God's holy wrath and cut his throat with a lightning bolt.

Skinner moved through dark and street glow past the poolrooms and the taverns, the seedy blue-lit lounges, down into the back alleys of the catacombs amidst the midnight prowl of shadows. No one went at night to No Man's Land. Even during the day you didn't want to go alone. You went after school in pairs or groups to your favorite trick to get your treat, clicking switchblades and looking mean. Hands in his pockets, sweating bullets, Skinner stumbled down the unlit streets, over the broken sidewalks, amidst the abandoned buildings, most of them fire-scorched shells, like they weren't in America but some third world war zone. *The hanging tree waits for me.* Skinner sang to himself tunelessly. Phantom figures stalked him. He didn't care. *Hanging tree, hanging tree.*

For the thousandth time, he reran the robbery in his mind. How scared he had been when he saw Camacho's gun. *"How else we gonna rob him? Say: 'Give me your money or I'll kick you in the shin?'"* They went in as soon as the old man opened. No customers then. They lifted their T-shirts over their noses, pulled down their hats, wore dark sunglasses. But the gun went off. *Boom.* Skinner had never seen anything like it, the way the old man dropped.

"If we repent and are serious and we beg God's forgiveness with all our heart and soul," Camacho put his arm around Skinner's shoulder as they patrolled the alley, *"God will forgive us, amigo. God wants to give us another chance. It was an accident. I'll get the gun. We won't go to prison."*

Was Camacho feeding him some jive, as if he was stupid? Maybe Camacho really believed all that bullshit? Camacho was not so bad. Camacho was his only friend. If it wasn't for Camacho, Skinner knew, he probably would be dead long ago. Eventually the gangs would have stomped him good. They had come pretty close more than once. Maybe they would have set him on fire with gasoline or whatever like the gangs did to that white kid in the news.

"What you doin' here white trash?" They surrounded him after his first day at school. Skinner's family moved to the neighborhood a year ago. *"You come to give me some money? No? I think maybe you better have some tomorrow."*

Skinner's father had lost his job. They lost their house, savings, everything. Both his parents worked in the packing plant now for minimum wage and were lucky to have that. The new life was a shock. They came from the suburbs, good schools, jobs. The more Skinner tried to fit in the worse it got. The gangs would taunt him, shake him down, beat him up – the blonde, blue eyed target. Now everyone left him alone. He hung with Camacho. *"Muy inteligente."* Camacho would pat Skinner on the back when they ran into his pack. *"A master mind."* Camacho would tap his temple. *"He gonna rob a bank with his brains and put you Frito banditos to shame."*

"Dealer." Skinner whispered and tapped at the sheet metal door across which *Death* was spray painted. The building was an old, brick, boarded up warehouse. The phantom shapes behind him ghosted away. "Dealer." He tapped harder.

"Nada más." A dark voice hissed. "Go away. We closed."

"It's Skinner." Skinner stammered. "Camacho's friend. You know – Blanco."

"Beat it."

"I got money. Plenty."

"Stick it up you ass."

"It's an emergency." Skinner pleaded. "Camacho sent me." He lied. "We got this party, these chicks. Camacho begs you."

Skinner had stolen a hundred dollars from his parents savings toward rent. He could sell the crack over the next few days and put it back. He was going crazy. He had to talk to Dealer. His mind was in a frenzy.

"How much is plenty?"

"A hundred?" Skinner held his breath.

"That's plenty? Shit!"

The door swung open. Looking at Dealer made you shudder. He had wild hair and a shock theater face, nose-ringed, eyebrow-ringed, the forehead, cheeks, chin slashed with zipper-like scars. His eyes could stare down a firing squad. Camacho had gotten the gun from him.

"Blanco."

Dealer swayed in the doorway and sneered at Skinner. He stood stark naked, holding a gun. His sinuous brown body shimmered with tattoos: devils, demons, screaming faces, snakes, magic numbers, voodoo writings.

"Let's have it." Dealer stuck out his hand. Skinner's pale one shook as he paid him. "Stay there." Dealer pointed at the doorstep with his gun. "Lilliana!" He turned and disappeared. "Bring me my box! It's in the closet!"

The room beyond the doorway looked like a psychopath's nightmare. Skinner had been in it with Camacho a few weeks ago. It was a huge, dimly lighted space. Somehow Dealer managed to reclaim part of the warehouse from extinction with plumbing and electricity. Miracles like that happened in the hood everywhere, mystery electricity, phone connections, cable TV. In the vast, warehouse space, naked light bulbs dangled from steel beams. The walls were painted with surrealistic street scenes in which giant, garishly colored figures, twisted in a hell that raged from floor to ceiling. Hell was the hood on fire. The jumble of toppling tenements and gaudy storefronts were whipped by flames and peopled with demons. In every building's windows, Hispanic families howled with torment. Dealer must have gotten the neighborhood graffiti artists in there and supplied them with paints and brushes. Their vision was a holocaust of despair and destruction. Dilapidated furniture was scattered throughout the room. In a corner there was a kitchen, television, computer, CD player. Beyond Dealer's torture chamber, blocked off by a maze of cinder brick walls, was a gutted shell filled with rubble and junk, inhabited by stray dogs, winos, druggies and rodents,

48

"Enjoy your blow." Dealer reappeared and tossed him a bag. "Don't do this no more, Blanco. Never. When I say 'no más' you get lost, fast."

"Dealer." Skinner stammered. "Can I ask you a question? I don't have a computer anymore so I can't look up the answer. Do guns attract lightning? I mean they're made of metal. I know cops wear guns everywhere. But say a cop stands by a tree in a storm. Trees get struck all the time. Would a gun increase the odds of lightning striking? If anyone would know you would. Dealer?"

Nights winds whispered around them in the tangled parish garden, like chanting saints or nuns at prayer. Or maybe it was more like midnight angels fluttering in the dark, or priests reciting sermons, or choirs caroling incantations. Sweet sis, the sensations on their skin as they kissed, bit, tangled with delight, naked in the garden moonlight.

"Bueno." Camacho groaned. He leaned over Juanita and searched her features, tasted he breath, felt her quiver. The heavens opened up on a world that is enough. "Bueno." He repeated. "Amen."

They had attended the night mass, knelt together, prayed, or at least Camacho did. It was his idea. He had showered after dinner, put on a silk shirt and new chinos, had an impulse to attend the service. "Oh, I don't know Julio." Juanita hesitated before the great doors of the grand cathedral with its ringing bells, towering steeple. "It doesn't seem right. We can't pray, then go out in the garden and – you know."

"It's OK." Camacho squeezed her hand. "We'll pray for a baby."

"I don't think so! I think I pray the other way! Julio you crazy!"

Darkness adorned with candlelight, silver and gold flickering in the shadows, stained glass windows that sparkled like jewels, sacred statues, the alter, the pulpit, the crucifix, the priest, alter boys, hallowed music, head bowed they closed their eyes and crossed themselves, silent before the holy rituals and mystical aura of a transcendent world.

Camacho had quit going to church long ago. He would pretend he went, saying to his parents that he would attend a later mass. He was too tired Sunday mornings from his week of school and wrestling practice. The mysteries of birth, death, living, dying, creation, sin, meant less and less to him as he grew up in the hood. *"Bless me Father for I have sinned."* What did that mean? He lived in a no man's land of stab and grab, where everyone was on the make, take, fake – not just the barrio but the whole country – everyone running around with their bag of tricks, rip-offs, tip-offs, payoffs, shakedowns. Where were the goodies in his Christmas stocking? He figured out real fast he had to fill it on his own. And it wasn't through worship and prayer – that never got anyone anywhere.

"If it's no good here," his father tapped his heart, *"it's no good anywhere."*

Camacho watched the priest perform the service and recalled the words of his father. It was true, his heart was no good anymore. He was as bad as the worst. He was a killer – just an old, miserly man at the end of his days but still he deserved to live and Camacho had taken his life away. *"What do you know about war, muchacho?"* His father had chided him. He knew rumbles, drive-bys, gang initiations, the dangers of the streets, and now he knew murder. Could he do it again if he joined the service? Killing felt different. He should kill Skinner, Camacho knew. Snap his neck and throw him off a viaduct before he chickened out and talked. There was no way he was going to spend the rest of his life in prison. Something had saved him, God, luck, the souls of his ancestors. A hand had reached out of the sky and grabbed his crime, hid it so he could get rid of it. Something had given him a chance to start again, maybe to do something grand. Could he let Skinner ruin that?

Skinner was his friend, his amigo, more than anyone else in the ghetto. He was the only reason Camacho hadn't flunked the school year. *"Let me show you some tricks."* He had sat down next to Camacho in class, after the teacher had humiliated him again. *"PEMDAS."* He wrote on a sheet of paper. *"This is a formula. It's like tips on how to wrestle, trips and flips. I'll explain how it works. What's important is to multiply or divide before you add, unless there's a parenthesis. Do these guys, exponents, first."* It was miraculous. Skinner was better than the teacher. He helped him with all the astronaut stuff too. Enough to get him through. *"Mi amigo! What would I do without you!"* What would he do with Skinner now? Skinner was a danger. He had to keep Skinner quiet one way or another.

Camacho looked at Juanita. Bonita Juanita with her eyes closed and hands folded. She had a hard life. She had dropped out of school to work at the plant. Her father had left them. Her mother worked the second shift, which was why Juanita could easily sneak out whenever he called. She had two little brothers and three younger sisters. She paid Carlotta, the oldest, to baby sit and keep her mouth shut.

"Get a job, get a wife, get a life." His father chided.

"Pretty one," Camacho whispered, "it's time for our communion."

"That Blanco loco!" Dealer stormed through the door. "That crazy anglo! You hear him? You hear him jabber at me about lightening and cops and guns and trees? I do his skinny white ass a favor and he babble like a mad man at me about computers and metal and lightening and drive me crazy!"

"Calm down Ramon. Sit here, smoke this." Lilliana gave him the joint she just lit. "I get you a nice cold beer. He just a loco anglo. Let it go."

"I keel him!" Dealer flopped back on the sofa and waved his gun. "I aim and pull the trigger but the safety's on! I get so mad I forget to take it off! I keel him!"

Lilliana returned with a beer. She snuggled up to him on the sofa and laid her head on his shoulder.

"Easy baby. Blanco gone now. No more Blanco."

"I rip out his gut! I cut off his nuts! Next time I see heem, that Blanco he a corpse!"

"Shh … shh …"

Guns and lightening and cops and trees, over and over – his brain was dizzy. Dealer imagined grabbing Skinner and slashing his throat, watching those blue eyes bug out, blood pour out of his jabbering mouth. "Un momento." He calmed down. "Un momento. Más tarde, más tarde." He took a sip of the cold beer and a drag off the joint. Guns and lightening, cops and trees. His eyes swept the wall across from the sofa. There was a sprawling tree painted near the door. A noose hung from it. "The tree of crime bears bitter fruit," was scrawled under it. He remembered the shooting a few days before. The old guy who owned the jewelry store. Rumor had it that the cops had hauled in two suspects but they couldn't pin it on them because they couldn't find the weapon. Blanco and Camacho? The gun he sold to Julio? Maybe they hid the gun in a tree? Crazy but maybe.

Dealer pondered this, trying to imagine how it could be done. Jump a fence and hang it on a branch, jump back and run? Dealer was a snitch. That's how he stayed in business. The cops let him operate for rumors, leads, names, tips. Now and then they would raid him, but it was just for show. He'd be out in the morning, shrugging it off, letting rumors spread around about his mystic powers and underground connections. A gun in a tree in a yard across the alley from the store. He'd make a call. Maybe it was nothing, but just trying would keep him in favor with the law.

Most nights, in the back of no man's land, where the tracks turned by the packing plants, hobo fires would toss around the shadows of homeless men Chicago bound. The freight trains slowed down there to round the bend in their final run to the city where a vagrant's paradise of missions, soup kitchens, and bustling streets where quick change could be hustled, lay waiting for the taking.

They would drop off there to avoid the risk of beatings and incarceration from railroad security for vagrancy, trespassing. They would take the CTA the rest of the way. When the snow came they'd be back again, heading south or west – those who weren't dead from bad booze, fights, or who had landed in prison.

The moon was gone. Black clouds closed over Camacho like the lid of a coffin. He sat on the roof of his sweltering tenement, drinking tequila and smoking cigarettes. Like a holy vision his mind revisited the Cathedral and Juanita – how they had lain side by side on a blanket of soft grass deep in the garden, two breathless shadows. The tangle of trees wove another cathedral above them as they cuddled, with a window on a dream of starlight and moon glow.

"Are you really there?" The night seemed to whisper. *"Yes we are, yes we are."* Was the answer.

Thunder boomed over the tenement rooftop. The winds picked up, blowing through the windows of the inferno below him like an angel's breath, soothing the bodies if not the souls of the dreamers who tossed in their slumbers.

Camacho watched the tiny, hobo fires shivering by the tracks beyond the catacombs. Maybe he would ride a train soon the other way – if it came to that. Could he let it come to that? Take one west where there was not so much law and there were a lot of Mexicans and he could blend in, get lost. There was a city of vagrants who lived under the storm drains of Las Vegas. He saw that on TV. Lots of people now were out on the streets. Who would pay attention to another homeless Mexican?

He imagined himself running alongside of a freight car, climbing in, another lost soul on a ghost train – running, hiding, begging maybe, stealing maybe, staying in flop houses, missions. He wasn't going to be caged in. He wasn't going to fight for his life everyday with sub-humans. Maybe he deserved it. Was he one of them? But what did anyone expect of him? He had spent his life watching everyone around him, family, friends, collect their junkyard dreams and pile them in a heap amidst the acid rains and tangled weeds of poverty. They expected him to live that way? It was an accident that he killed the old man. But he would make up for it someday. That's what the miracle tree was all about. At least that's what he felt in his heart: *make amends, start again, do something noble, worthy, serve his country, save lives, give up his own if necessary.*

Skinner. Camacho brooded. He twisted the bottle around in his hands.

Thunder rumbled across the blackened city, lightening flared. The dark, desolate buildings zigzagged through a nightmare. Skinner crossed the deserted ghetto furtively. Although no one was there, he felt he was being shadowed everywhere.

"I keel you!"

Dealer had screamed, pointing the gun at him.

He stumbled out of the catacombs, staggered home, more confused than ever. Everyone was asleep. His parents drank now heavily. They lived in a daze, working double shifts for minimum wage. His younger sisters were druggie sluts, all made up. Before you knew it, they'd both be knocked up. *"Hey Blanco, last night I boom boom you seester. You no like it? Maybe you want to do something about it?"*

He hid the crack behind his dresser, sat in the dark in a frenzy looking for the answer. Maybe they should both go in and confess? They hadn't taken anything. They ran. They were in shock. It was an accident, kind of like reckless driving. The cops had no suspects. If they did the right thing and went in, spilled their guts, the authorities should be willing to cut them some slack – serve a little time, go on parole, rehabilitation. But he knew it wouldn't work. They would need a high-priced mouthpiece to pull that off. That was rich kid stuff, suburbia. Everyone knew they threw the book at inner city fuck ups.

He got a flashlight from the kitchen and went out again. He felt like a ghost in a dream as he moved down the lightening-lit streets, along the pitch black alleys and the crypt-like gangways, stepping over broken bottles, stumbling over piles of trash. This was not his world. He couldn't even read the writings on the billboards and buildings. Now it was his nightmare even more than before. *"I keel you! I keel you!"* He couldn't stand it anymore. He wanted to go to college, be an engineer. His dream was to work on the space program, be part of conquering the new frontier. The new frontier? He was back in the middle ages. War lords, drug lords, turf wars, misery, poverty, murders, robberies – Iran, Iraq, Afghanistan, the barrio, what was the difference? Instead of exploring the stars he faced a life behind bars. But he didn't do anything! Camacho brought the gun. He didn't want to rat out Camacho. But what did the code of silence have to do with him? What did any of this have to do with him? He was white trash in ghetto land. They would have killed him long ago if he hadn't played along, made friends with Camacho. But would Camacho have been his friend if he hadn't helped him? No way José! But that wasn't really fair. Their friendship went deeper than that now. There had gotten to be something inexplicable between them, something close, important.

Skinner could see nothing. The city was erased. The only way he found the jewelry store alley was through flashes of lightening. The sprawling tree was waving its branches in the wind. It looked like some sci-fi movie monster menacing the world amidst flares, rumbles and explosions of blinding light that erupted with the storm.

"They got a dog, amigo." Camacho was suddenly standing beside him holding a bottle of tequila. "Big, black, ugly, ferocious – a hound from hell." He took a swig from his bottle and squinted at the lashing downpour. "It's chained to the tree. It can cover the whole yard. It lives in a little house right next to it. 'Casa no trespassa.' It's in there now. It gave up trying to eat me when I moved away from the yard." Camacho downed the rest of the bottle and tossed it in the trash. He wiped his mouth with the sleeve of his rain soaked silk shirt. "You got a flashlight. Bueno." He clicked on his. "We do some tricks of math, amigo. Multiply, divide, subtract. You go over to the end of the fence and attract the demon. When he try to kill you, I hop over and climb the tree. That gun got to be stuck in some thick branch by the tree's trunk. When I get up on a limb I shout at Satan. When he come after me it's your turn. That grande tree too much for me. You come around back and I pull you up. How do we get down? Maybe we have to subtract the demon with the gun.

Skinner's heart pounded as he listened to Camacho. The air had cooled dramatically and he felt a chill shiver over his rain soaked body. He remembered the first time the gang had surrounded him after school. He felt a fear like that come over him now. He felt trapped, surrounded and there was no way out.

"Let's do it." Skinner tapped Camacho with his flashlight.

"Bueno! The Alamo! Mexican standoff, amigo!"

Skinner crossed the alley tensely and moved along the fence. He tapped on it with his flashlight, bracing his body for an attack. It was as if the night had transformed into a creature, exploding thunder and flashing death. The dog flew at him from out of nowhere, snarling, growling, snapping as it tugged fiercely at the chain which bound it to the tree. Skinner almost dropped his flashlight. The sudden shock of the monster caught his breath. For an instant he was staring into the mad dog eyes of Dealer. *I keel you! I keel you!* Just as suddenly the demon disappeared.

Real time was dream time – staccato images captured in flashes of lightening. Skinner saw in cosmic blinks Camacho trying to shimmy up the tree drunkenly, slipping, leaping, grabbing at a branch. He saw the bolting dog lunge at him. They were on the ground. Camacho wrestled him off. He leaped for the tree again. The dog was tarring at his leg.

"Aii Chihuahua!" Camacho licked at the dog's mouth. "You ain't no Chihuahua!" He grabbed a branch and pulled himself up. His pants leg was ripped to shreds. He felt blood oozing from his calf. "Maybe I should let you eat Skinner, monster, maybe it would make my life simpler?" He sat on the branch and shined the light on the leaping dog below. It was a big one, at least a hundred pounds. Eyes blazing, it clawed and snapped, snarled and growled, determined to bite the foot off his dangling leg. "Hey Devil!" He shouted down. "When I get my gun I shoot you in the ass! What you think about that!" Camacho wondered why the old couple needed such a beast. Maybe they had money hidden in their mattress? Muy interesante. Oh well, he was done with that.

"Psst!" Skinner was behind him reaching for the branch. Camacho swung around, reached down, and grabbed him by the hand. "I thought that demon was going to see me!" Skinner rasped and shoved a tangle of leaves away as Camacho pulled him up. "I don't know how I made it!" He settled down on a neighboring branch.

"No, he too much busy trying to kill me. Beside, Blanco, you too skinny."

It was like a clown circus act, the two of them trying to keep their balance as they stood up and beamed their flashlights on the tossing limbs and branches. The tree pitched and swayed and swung its leafy limbs at them; but at least it kept the downpour off them. They divided the tree between them, circling around its trunk. They moved across and back, up and down, shining their flashlights all around, crisscrossing, colliding. "Man, I couldn't have thrown that gun this high!" Camacho whispered. "I know we should have found the fucking thing by now." It seemed like daylight when lightening lit the sky. One flash was so bright it was blinding. The thunder that followed was like the explosion of a canon. They had to hold on to one another to keep from falling. "Can you see anything?" Skinner blinked. "Only shooting stars amigo and cross-eyed moonbeams."

Sometimes Skinner was above him, sometimes below. Sometimes he disappeared in the leaves altogether and suddenly Camacho would find him standing right behind him. "This is loco my friend." "I know." They could no longer hear the barking dog. They could no longer see the ground below. The rain stopped. They had climbed above the clouds. The stars looked like basketballs.

"Where are we going Camacho?"

Skinner sat on a branch and looked down at the spinning earth in a trance.

"I don't know." Camacho kept climbing. "Maybe heaven, amigo."

BEGGAR

Staggering stranger,
I've walked barefoot
through hell.
I've laughed, cried at
prayers. In the midst
of my sin, I've been a saint, helping
others. I've slayed a dragon or two,
saved a soul now and then.
I'm not sure what
I'm trying to tell you.
I'm a man, simply.
No man is an island.

UNDER THE TABLE

Big odds. I make out pretty good,
at least today. Easy to explain. I got
a tip from my buddy Jake. He junks
the horses at the track now and then.
We go back. Sometimes he cuts me in.
Suppose he could do it more often.
I can't complain. Never did expect
to live the American Dream.
No. Now and then the world slides
away from me. Messes with my ways
and means. Hard to keep my balance,
stay on my feet.
I'm no fool. I dimmed the lights, closed
the curtains, shut the door long ago.
when I first felt the jinx grab my throat.
I keep to the shadows, try not to mix
it up too much. Tempts bad luck. Like
I say I'm no fool. I look around and
What do I see? Big odds coming at me.

NOT INCLUDED

Rainy afternoon, everything lost. At least
it felt that way to Lonigan, even though he
had managed to find another job. Nothing
nearly as good as the one he lost: a small
plant that made batteries.
It paid half of what he was making at the
factory. Still he was lucky. Many of his
friends still weren't working. The
lingering Recession was disturbing.
Lonigan sipped his beer. He was supposed
to be celebrating. Instead he kept
studying his reflection in the mirror,
pondering the damage that had been done by
the years: the creases in his face, receding
hair. Still he looked pretty good … however
he was middle-aged and poor, horny, lonely,
divorced.

Lucky he and Judy didn't have kids. He'd be
trying to earn child support to pay for the
privilege of being a father on weekends.
We can't win. Lonigan told his
reflection. Which made him a loser, he
supposed. That's the way life goes. But the
economy was picking up, so who knows?

"Hemlock on the rocks."
Lonigan looked at the woman who sat down
a stool away from him.

"Hemlock?" The bartender grinned.

"Beats getting crucified again."

The woman took off her floppy rain hat.

She was pretty, thirty-something, blonde.

"It's death by a thousand shots in here."

The bartender said. "We don't serve anything
that strong."

"Then let's get going. A double bourbon."

"This one's on me." Lonigan lifted his mug.

"I'm celebrating."

"Congratulations." She studied Lonigan.

"That's refreshing. Good news in a Recession.
I'll drink to your good fortune."

"My pleasure. I finally found a job. Battery
maker. Pays half as much as I made before.
Mind if I move over?"

"OK. You can tell me more about batteries
and the Energizer Bunny."

"And shoes and ships and ceiling wax,"
Lonigan joined her, "cabbages and kings."

"And why the world turned upside down."

"And can we ever turn it around again?"

THE TIMES, THEY ARE DERANGING

Bad times when falling angels fill the sky
like carnival confetti for the devil's delight.
Bad times when nothing jives and the same
lame lies pass like valentines among the
cubicle people in their sitcom lives.
Bad times when the wind cries toxic moans
as the planet dies.
"The cause of your misfortune is apparent."
Says an official of the corporate establishment.
"Your errant mind is completely aberrant."
Candlelit skulls light the windows of the tenements.
Corpses chant mantras throughout the labyrinths. Each
day shoots for the moon, lands on vampire bat wings.
"Poverty is a privilege not a privation."
Says the official from the corporation.
"'tis the lifeblood of a mighty nation."
Bodies float down a river of blood –
orphans, runaways, suicides, fallen soldiers,
the lame, sick, halt and blind in a survival
of the fittest where only the empowered thrive.
In a cellar window a wizened widow eats dog
food from a can at a three-legged table.
Bad times when peace is war,
homeless shelters are closed for the poor,
tax cuts for the rich increase,
jobs are outsourced overseas,
up is down, wrong is right, and you're
in between nowhere and no way out.
Sewers run to the sea, wait for me.

LIFER

Like the death moan of a hopeless Brontosaurus,
choking on fog and sinking into prehistoric darkness,
the noon whistle blows its agonized drone over the
docks, lines, mills, bins, tech shops, foundries, smoke-
smothered labyrinths.
Legions of laborers, dressed in blue, green, gray work drabs,
pour out of the industrial buildings from every direction.
The mass march maneuvers through the maze in a sun-dazzled
lockstep, swelling, mingling, massing, merging, doggedly shuffling,
until they dead-end at the cafeteria's jam-packed entrance.
Every day, I imagine that I'm in a Hollywood penal flick –
"The House Of Numbers," or "Alcatraz," or on cold, rainy days
Fritz Lang's spooky, silent movie "Metropolis."
It didn't feel that way before they cut our pay, pensions,
health care, vacation days. I guess we're all just serving out
sentences here, anyway, like I've heard some preachers say.

CROSSED

Star or Double –
that's what it's come to,
at least here in America,
where the disparity between
the haves and the have-nots
gets bigger every year.
The rich grab everything.
The middle class take the rest.
The poor get what's left,
next to nothing at best.
In Canada, Scandinavia, Europe,
the Netherlands, Israel, parts of
Latin America and Asia, all the
socially-minded democracies,
things are better. In these countries
the middle class is growing not
shrinking. Half of this country is
living in or near poverty.
Most of the rest are waiting to join
them, due to outsourcing, automation,
shrinking paychecks, jobs with no
benefits, computerization, dirty politics,
the one percent, and then some, not
paying their fair share of the tax burdens.
I got mine. They got theirs. Go get
yours. Vote. Vote smart, for yourself,
your families, your interests, every
time, and you'll survive. Actually,
you'll thrive.

BLOW THE MAN DOWN

One foot in the gutter, the other the grave,
the days pass in a haze. Each sentence a
word game scrambling for meaning in my brain.
Body the same, rubbery legs trying to navigate
a sidewalk which rocks like the deck of a
battleship. (Too late to avoid falling through
those cracks from which you never come back.)
While the blur of what was, is only recalled
in blinks between drinks.
The blur of what is stinks, but in many ways
it's better than that time I could recognize the
pain in my own and other's eyes: that world-
weary expression, those looks of desperation
which became more hopeless each day of the
never-ending recession
It was the same look of despair I saw each
morning in the mirror before I found the magic
potion that made it all disappear.
Once I had an office, a small business that
thrived. A welcome stillness amidst the madness
of existence, where I could gaze out the window
at the small park below, watch it rain, watch it
snow, watch the wind blow through the trees as
we lived above our means trying to grab our
share of the American Dream – a futile enterprise.
Even without an economic catastrophe, the country
can bring you to your knees.
Once I had a family, kids and a wife, friends
and colleagues.
Once I had a silver cigarette case. Once I was
part of the human race.

LABOR BREAK

Working the night shift,
the stars glitter and
the moon glows in the dimly-
lit factory window, making
the midnight production seem
peaceful and serene.
The glow will keep me going
'til dawn. The recession is still
going on. I'm lucky to
have this job. Not much
of one but at the end of its
run every morning there's
you, the kids,
my daily homecoming.

CLOCKERS

We rotate shifts every week
here, from first to third in a
continuous progression, so no
one is ever quite sure what's
going on with their bodily
functions. Morning, midnight,
the moon at noon? Your head
gets in a mess. Makes life even
more of a dream than it would
ordinarily be as a cog in a
machine, repeating the same
function over and over again,
with no concept of time to
keep things in equilibrium.
It's supposed to be good for
production. Bodies in motion
with no brain to distract them.
Morale too, because everyone
gets to grab their share of that
OT pay for time working those
shifts when the rest of the world
is at play or in bed or having a
beer and watching a ballgame.
Got to hand it to the executives.
Way to go, geniuses! I'll give
them a thumbs up next time I'm
working the nine to five and get
to see them. Hope I remember
to make the correct gesture.
Things get mixed up, more now
than ever.

TROUBLE TOWN 1

Desperate years descending,
no time to play dead.
Fog covers the American
cities, chokes what
life is left.
A circus of lies and alibis,
time seems to slip away,
disappears with your years,
takes you to your grave.
The recession is over, or
at least not as severe.
The roof tops glisten with
rain washing away our
fears. Candles glow in
many windows, signs of
hope we all hold dear.

REX SEXTON

MOUNT MONEY

From the backstreet brothels in third
world countries, in those murky cellars
or filthy hovels, where the profits from
child's play aren't made from selling
lemonade and the boxes of goodies
don't refer to girl scout cookies ...
From the underworlds and
netherworlds of warlords, drug
lords, tyrants, gangsters ...
From the under-the-table entrepreneurs ...
From the under-the-radar market
manipulators ... money flows into the
banks of Switzerland, where see, hear,
speak no evil is the mantra of a neutral
people.
It's a beautiful country: snowcapped
mountains, pristine lakes, each city a
little diamond, perfect for vacationing.
We feel at home there, fit right in,
because we're neutral too, Americans,
once we get ours that is: jobs, healthcare,
a way and means to live. Those of us
who haven't are not our concern. God
helps those who help themselves, is our
saying.
Even if he doesn't it's no skin off our
noses. They can always fight our abundant
wars – the young ones anyway. That will
get them healthcare and pay, a roof over
their heads, even a pension if they live.

70

I guess we're a lot like the Swiss.
Except, of course, for the social programs
they have to take care of their citizens
from cradle to grave, which goes against
our grain.

REX SEXTON

OUR TOWN II

The streets, here, remember nothing
that matters. Night and day, the
pounding of machinery from the
smoke-stacked factories, punctuated
by the rumble of freight trains, is the
dream-stream that babbles through
your brain from waking to sleeping,
and in a muffled way, dreaming to
waking. Funerals, weddings, the
patriotic holiday festivities, vary them,
now and then, with small gatherings
of working class men, women and their
children. But they quickly return to their
ghost-walked dead ends, amidst clouds
of smoke and bunkered down residents.
These are mean streets, at best, lost in an
existential forgetfulness, much diminished
from the times that created them, when
hard labor brought enough pay to enrich
them – days when the incessant pounding
didn't take its toll on your soul because at
the end of each your life had something to
show. These are streets which no longer
care to remember, but occasionally
reminisce about the good old days and
tales of lost bliss. Memories, here, are
like pennies now, all from heaven, of
course, because life is precious, yet at
the same time worthless. One each day,
perhaps for your thoughts, which you

lose as you collect them to the wishing
wells of Time's misfortune, dreaming of
other streets you might have walked, long
ago, when legend proposed they were
paved with gold.

THE NOT OK CORRAL

Drifting off, rain pounding the leaky roof
of the Crystal Palace, jukebox broke.
This sweltering night is all but over.
I'll leave it in a stupor, stagger home
down busted backstreets, over broken glass,
cracked concrete, amidst the rotting remnants
of torched buildings some slumlord set
ablaze for insurance.
I try to remember better days. I look in the bar
mirror and shake my head. Those times when
going to work meant making a living not
just surviving.
This ain't no palace in case you were
wondering. Never saw any crystal in here
either – no sparkling glassware or chandeliers.
This is just a Chi-town dive. It was named
by the crazy owner after some famous cowboy
bar in Wichita, Kansas. Wyatt Earp used to
drink there, I hear.
Most of us are just trying to make it through
the summer. Those of us who do will have to
face the winter. There ain't no Miss
Kitty in here neither, nor anything like her.
What we got, instead, is why God invented
darkness.
They'll never fix that jukebox.

SLEEPWALKING

Remnants of wreckage tangled
together, Franklin Foster wanders
the downtown streets in tatters.
Mouth open, feet dragging, pale
eyes staring, horns blaring, as he
ghosts across the busy intersections.
Franklin remembers falling, screaming,
howling in his nightmare, arms
flailing, legs kicking, clutching,
grasping, plunging. Finally he
awakened. Nothing was clear,
as Franklin slowly picked himself up
from the gutter, neither the past
nor the present, nor the future.
The future? Franklin almost remembers
a line by Shakespeare, something
about day to day in a petty pace?
Other memories emerge, shadowy,
fleetingly – faces, places. All gone
with those winds of time that life
erases. The crowds bustle past.
Like a ghost in a dream, Franklin Foster
shadows through the flow, a step
at a time, although he has nowhere
to go.

TICKET TO RIDE

The moon was gone. Black clouds closed
over the city like the lid of a coffin.
Thunder boomed and the winds picked up,
blowing through the windows of the inferno
below him like an angel's breath, soothing
the body, not the soul. That would always
stay trapped in Hell.
Tim sat on the roof of his sweltering tenement.
He watched the tiny, hobo fires shivering by
the tracks beyond the slums, that dark jumble
of buildings falling down.
He imagined himself running alongside a
freight car as the train slowed to make
its turn, grabbing a rung and climbing on,
another lost soul on a ghost train, going
nowhere, going anywhere, ghost town bound,
maybe not tonight but soon.
Staccato images of hardscrabble slum life
flash before him with the lightning,
a battle no one can win, or survive, not without
becoming more dead than alive.
"Nowhere" was better than here.
Anywhere was better than here.
Anything was better than nothing, and here
nothing was all there was for him.

BORN TO LOSE

Like a death rattle of wind chimes
playing the desperate cries of hard
times, through dark, despairing notes
across the shivering rhythms of their
hearts and souls, the lost generation
wanders the recession, searching for
salvation from life's regression, hoping
too little, too late won't come from
whatever can change their fate.
It's the music sensation that's sweeping
the nation – the beat of a dream's retreat.
You can hear it in Chicago, in the Motor
City, in Philadelphia, PA, Kansas City,
down in New Orleans, all across the
country

WHEN YOU WISH I

A sleepless night – in the darkness Becker
thought about the cold, tomblike blackness.
He thought about his empty life, from
family man to nowhere man overnight.
In truth it took some time. Years of
flying blind.
Jobless, holed up in a cheap flat,
started last week when Carol left him
and the corporation dropped him. They
could have put him into prison for embezzling.
The old man let it go. Over the years they
had gotten close, almost like father and son.
Becker was a great disappointment to him.
Movies, dreams, life is wished for in these –
but never achieved. The rarified dazzles the
eye like clouds floating by.
Becker got dazzled – big job, money, almost
sky is the limit for his business expenses.
He was burning the candle at both ends,
even before he got into casino gambling.
Becker sighed and thought about women.
He had plenty of them. They came with
the tailored suits and Mercedes Benz.
How good it would be to be lying next to
a soft body to keep him warm. Carol and
not a siren would be the best. But she took
the kids and left.
Life was a clunky work-a-day copy of that

rarified reality.
Becker wanted it back.
He wanted to get his life back on track.
But that train was gone, never coming back.

REX SEXTON

WHEN YOU WISH II

Spirit gone,
world all wrong,
inside out,
upside down,
blowing bubbles,
bubbles burst,
Fantasia ride in Disneyland over ...
"Bar's closed."
"One for the road."
"You've had an 'extra' two."
"I'm not through."
"Time to go home!"
"One more and I'm gone!"
Bubble, bubble, toil and trouble ...
Mickey Mouse bought a house for
Minnie and Sleeping Beauty and
Cinderella and little Jiminy.
"Don't you have a home?"
Next stop the Twilight Zone.

THE BIG CHILL

Days bleak, bitter, with the early
onslaught of winter,
no heat in the building, night coming
quickly, wife stoic, kids colic, "holding
money" gone with the economy,
I prowl ghostly streets, past shut down
workshops, factories.
No going back to what was before,
because it isn't there anymore.

CONSTANT IS THE RAIN

Being and begetting, struggling and
enduring, all of it bewildering as time
passes and the church bells ring.
Like cold rain running through her
veins, the chilling feeling as Delphi
walks the ghetto streets each day,
shivering even when the sun is
blazing. While across the city
where the girls her age look so
pretty, strolling in their fashionable
clothes along the tree lined lanes
and avenues, is where she prays
she'll live someday, somehow,
someway.
Shadows stalk her shivering steps.
Life shifts through a freezing mist,
as gunfire crackles and sirens wail
and her fate is sealed with coffin nails.

YESTERDAY

Back of the Battery sprawled a
blue collar badlands which often
proved deadly. Train yards
loaded with freight cars, a maze
of narrow crisscrossing streets
cluttered with small shops, plants
and factories, pubs, bars, seedy lounges
all embedded amidst our humble,
rickety, dilapidated dwellings, turned
this tract of urban blight into
a brawling, hard-drinking challenge
for any night.
Big Red, Tall Paul, Slim Jim, Fat Pete,
The Brago Brothers, the Dempsy
Brothers, it was fight or flight
everywhere you looked, every step
you took.
How did I fair? I didn't make
it out of there without a police record
− grand theft auto, burglary, dealing,
shoplifting, assault and battery.
It came with the trouble
town territory. It
could have been worse. I
could have bought it from a
bullet early on,
like many of my friends.

NEVER-NEVER LAND

The room is like a coffin,
sleep a death-dream of
childhood delirium,
sweating, tossing, running,
hiding …
"Come in from the night."
A voice says from behind a
door the kid has never seen before.
The night. The night.
Outside the sounds of the
dead zone abound: sirens,
gunshots, screams of terror.
"Come in from the night."
The voice says.
Never never is the
ghetto's answer.

" BACK ROADS "

There was this old dirt road in the little town of Jefferson that ended at a railroad track, dead ended right into it. I followed it thinking it would go somewhere. There weren't many places to go in Jefferson. It was an adventure. I never could figure out why the road went or stopped there. Had to be an explanation. I would have asked the townies more about it but I decided to stay out of it. I was the stranger who drifted into town, got a job at the lumber mill. Fresh out of high school, or there about, and looking around, trying to find my way in the world, figure things out.

Actually, I knew my way in the world, I figured out how to stay in it too. I was dodging the draft, keeping out of 'Nam. I already had friends maimed, mutilated, killed in those jungles. I'd move, inform the draft board. Move on. Meanwhile they kept sending notices to my home. I told my parents not to open them. I was trying to wait the war out. I did this for three years. The war went on for ten. You figure the odds on that one.

I already been given a medical draft deferment. But it ran out. Drugging, drinking, partying all night, waiting to get drafted I guess, we all were, I had contracted spinal meningitis. I was given last rights, flat-lined in a hospital, pronounced dead, came to with this whole experience of traveling through some other dimension.

I never got out of that other dimension. For years after, I had premonitions of all my friends who were killed and crippled in 'Nam. I dreamed of them, suffered their fear and agony, waiting for the news. If I got to 'Nam it would be worse. I'd be right in the middle of it. It would drive me nuts. The war was wrong anyway, Innocents being slaughtered for money on both sides. I couldn't get myself to fight in or for it.

Jobs were easy to get back then. They paid well too, not like generation X, Y and Z are doing. Our parents fought for unions. We fought to keep them. We all should have done more to prevent stupid wars. The unions died. Wars are constant now. All we do is backslide.

At noon everyday an old freight train would make its run through Jefferson and the neighboring towns. It would stop at the lumber yard. We'd load it up. There were chicken farms, dairy farms, a giant scrap junkyard owned by a Jew said to be the richest guy in the county. There were grain, egg, orchard distributers. Loading the train car with lumber was my cue to go to lunch. I'd stop at the diner for a burger and a coke, drive down the dirt road to where it met the tracks. Wait for the freighter to rumble past. The greatest show on earth as far as Jefferson went. It rattled round the bend, squeaking on its rusty wheels, whistle blasting. It was like a jolt of whisky, a hit of heroin. Its claptrap boxcars were hauling munchkins to wonderland. And then it was gone.

Like all small towns Jefferson was lacking in diversity, complexity, curiosity, ingenuity and, when you came right down to it, empathy and humanity. There was the town square, the Courthouse with the steeple, main street with its shops and stores, the movie theater. Heartland America. White America where conformity ruled. Everyone was for the war. The war was good. Protesters were cowards, feminists were troublemakers, civil rights advocates were angling for more white handouts and unjustified powers. Gay rights? Human rights? At whose expense – the religious rights'?

I moved on. Kept to myself. I got stopped for a traffic ticket in LA. My draft notice popped up. I was entrusted to the army. The army sent me to work for DIA (Defense Intelligence Agency). Gave me a Top Secret clearance. Why? I had nothing to do with it. But we were done with Vietnam, I soon learned. Although it would take many more years to run down there. The military devoted its time to preparing for a war, many wars, in the desert. Sand proof, heat proof equipment and machinery. Missiles and systems. I was involved in satellite tracking and information but I rarely focused on 'Nam. It was all about oil. Iraq, Arabia, Iran. I was shocked. It was an eye opener the way things worked. The political map in America is getting more mixed now. More people of color have come on to the scene trying to get their share of the American dream. Let's hope they are smarter than the white people from whom they've taken over.

Maybe that road to a dead end in Jefferson had a hidden warning. If we keep driving down stupid lane we'll get hit by a train?

"DREAMLAND"

Hard wind, everything tossing, chains snapping, cars rocking, Tanner shut down the Hell Bound, looked around: Dreamland a delirium of flying coffins. *"Fucking Jim."* Tanner searched the labyrinths. *"Fucking Jim."*

The dream lanes were jammed – the usual midsummer night's bedlam: trailer park vamps in their short shorts, beehive bouffants, more makeup on their doe-eyed faces than on a circus clown's (each of them promising their own wild ride for a box of popcorn and some cotton candy on the side), the townie gangs looking for different thrills than the amusement park could provide with its danger rides, the working class couples and their kids from the prefab housing developments around the industrial districts, the ethnics from the city's edge, as awed as if they found Shangri-la or Alice's Wonderland, the designer drug Goths double dosing on the carnie lights and circus trimmings, plus, grifters, pickpockets, perverts, whores, drug pushers, panhandlers and the too numerous to classify odds and ends strolling alone or together through the land of never-never, where, if he didn't move quick, might make "never" forever for some unlucky reveler.

Tanner shouldered through the mayhem, everyone around him enjoying the big wind as if it were an added attraction, laughing, screaming with glee as they clung to one another and ducked the flying debris, arcade tents flapping, café tables tumbling. *"Fucking Jim."* Rides awry, storm clouds chased across the sky. *"Man, you better get moving."*

"Shut it down!"

Tanner shouted at the gangly kid operating the Flying Squadron.

"Where's Jim?"

Wild-eyed, the skinny kid gaped at him.

"Shut it down. You'll kill someone!"

The mock planes were rocking, dipping as they whirled on their lines, veering with the gusts into the branches of the giant trees, which were everywhere, and made the "*amusement park a park*" according to the old man who refused to cut them down, despite the numerous warnings and frequent safety citations, which he bribed his way out of and were seasonally forgotten.

"Chain them!" Tanner hollered. "Chain them when you're done!"

The kid stared at him, blankly.

"They got anchor hooks on the bottom!"

"Because of the wind," Tanner brooded, *"the wind ..."*

They were in for a big one. *"The big blow from Kooky mo."* as Jim called it, the winds sweeping across the plains along tornado lane, which gave the windy city down the highway its stormy nickname. Jim, Stacey, the old man should have seen it coming (like on TV?) and done something.

"Move!" Tanner shouted and the kid almost jumped out of his skin. "Now! *"Hope you don't end up in my platoon, simpleton."* Tanner brooded, as his thoughts flashed back to the day he had gotten himself into this mess.

"This summer you're a danger runner." Jim had handed him a beer and informed him when they opened for the season. *"If you want. Tagart's off to Iraq. Joined over the winter.*

"Says he can't wait to get there, although he was hoping for Afghanistan. Itching to serve anywhere. He'll change his mind when the bullets start to fly. You know the drill: when the big blow comes shut the danger rides down. Yours first, of course," Jim waved his can of beer.

"Then help with the rest. Twister anywhere around, we close the park down – or anything near as fierce. You know how these summer

storms get around here: monsoon rain, lightning and thunder, bar the door and duck for cover. Buck and Whitey round out the crew. But I'm counting on you. I assume you know the pay raise for your upgrade in responsibility and authority: zero. That's the old man for you, thinks I can be everywhere. In other words you're a volunteer. It'll ruin your summer; so if it's a no can do I ain't blamin' you."

"Zero and a beer." Tanner had lifted his can in the air.

"I knew I had me a sucker here. Bet Uncle Sam's got one too. Suppose you'll be joining like Tagart now that you're through with school?"

"I been talkin' to the recruiter." Tanner had stiffened. *"But I'll finish the season. That's no problem."*

"Young men and heroism." Jim had shaken his head. *"When will it ever end?"*

"You joined for Nam." Tanner had reminded him. *"You won a decoration."*

"You don't win nothin' in war son. You only lose. War changes you. Besides, they were draftin' then. They would have got me in the end."

"There ain't no jobs, Jim. That's kind of like draftin'. I don't see any end to this recession." (*And I ain't going to get anywhere working here. That's for sure!*) Tanner had added to himself as he downed his beer.

The Hell Bound, the Flying Squadron, the Spinning Jenny and the Ferris Wheel, the Parachute, the Merry-go-round – six rides where a strong wind could hurt someone. Whitey had quit; Buck didn't show up for work. Without Jim he was on his own. There was no way Tanner could close the danger rides alone. They were too spread out and with this wind anything could happen in a split second. *"Two down, four to go. You got to move fast."* Jim had warned him.

"The crowds are the hang up. Knock someone down if you have to. They'll be OK. Better than havin' some guy take a high dive from the Parachute or Ferris Wheel."

90

Rides of every kind spinning before his eyes, crisscrossing, cascading, dropping, climbing, intertwining – Scrambler, Roller Coaster, Tilt-a-Whirl – fifty altogether, making him dizzy as he pushed through the mobs, all scattered amidst a forest and connected by a maze of lanes that would drive a laboratory rat insane. Tanner could hardly remember, on any given day, exactly where the rides were, or anything for that matter. The maze went every which way.

You could get lost in the Dream Lanes. Plus, they were as mad as a Mardi Gras in New Orleans, filled with barker booths, game galleries, arcades, fireworks, everything topsy-turvy – Spin the Wheel, Shoot the Ducks, Ring the Bell, Pitch the Penny, Dunk the Clown, Fool the Wizard, Knock Down the Bottles, See the Giant, Midget, Bearded Lady, while crazy calliope music played on speakers throughout the mayhem: "Carousel," "Home on the Range," "Meet Me in Saint Louis," "Waiting for the Robert E. Lee," "In the Good Ole Summertime," "Sidewalks of New York," mixed with heavy metal and acid rock. If you didn't get dizzy enough from the rides, the relentless music would blow your mind.

"The old man designed the park hisself." Jim had informed him when he first hired on three summers ago during his first high school break and Jim showed him around. *"Can't ya tell?"* That made instant sense and explained a lot. His first impression of the old man, when he shook his hand, was that the amusement park owner was as mad as a Hatter. He certainly cut a fine, distinguished figure with his snow-white, designer cut hair and clothes you only saw in movies about millionaires. But his sky-blue eyes looked hypnotized, as though they were looking, not at Tanner, but through him and beyond him and Tanner was just something in the way, which confused and amused him, while something way deep in the back of his mind was what consumed him. *"He designed some of the rides, too."* Hands in the pockets of his faded jeans, head bowed, massive shoulders rounded, staring at the ground, Jim had given him the lowdown, as they strolled

around, drawing him in with his drawl and creating a bond between them, man to man, which was probably something he learned how to do in Nam when he needed his men to back him. *"The Hell Bound and the Flying Squadron to name a few. Hell, he had a hand in most everything from the Tunnel of Love to the Pony Rides and the Magic Rings. Maybe you noticed, the park has a strong flavor of war to it all? There's the Combat Zone computer arcade and the motor boats which he calls Destroyers, and, of course, the Rifle Range. The old man was a bomber pilot during Nam. He bombed Hanoi, Laos, Cambodia, an assortment of ports and villages along the coast. He dropped Agent Orange on jungles, dropped Napalm. He was a frequent flyer whose distinctions for missions couldn't have been higher. We met there in between his runs and my adventures with shooting "Gooks" with guns. That's why I'm here. I was just a punk kid, not even eighteen, younger than you. He was an officer and a gentleman but somehow we got along. We met in a bar enjoying whores and liquor. His dream was Dreamland even way back then. He had it all planned and I was in, at least as the foreman. He must of got the idea for the park with every city he blew up and every forest he burned. Maybe I'm haunted in a way by every enemy soldier I shot. But I can see him up there with his wizard eyes gleamin' and dreamin'. I think he wanted to turn all that horror around, make something scary but fun and no harm to anyone. Don't we all. War is hell, son. I wish I had me a magic wand that could erase it all. This is his land. His parents left it to him, used to be a farm. There's a big house at the end which he lives in. Looks like another fairytale from Dreamland. You may have noticed it drivin' down the highway. It's hard to miss. He entertains all the big wigs there, political, industrial. He never had me and Beth over, but he sure likes to drop around our little shack in the winter when the season's over. Brings a bottle of the best. We talk about Nam, whores and war and how lucky we got outta there. He's a strange one. I don't know if I owe him everything or nothing. I've been in on this thing since day one. Job, shack. I think the main reason I'm here is so the old man can look back."*

That wasn't true from what Tanner knew. The old man couldn't have gotten the park off the ground without Jim around. They were wild times back then, thirty-five years ago. The area was unincorporated. You had to depend on the state police to keep the peace. They were few and far between. Jim was the enforcer. Tanner knew all about Jim from his father. *"You workin' where? Can't you get a job as a stock boy or grocery clerk? That's a lowdown, lowlife carnie world and the guy you'll be workin' for is a psycho killer. Yeah he was a hero in Nam.*

But I went there, too, and I didn't come back with my screws loose. That place will corrupt you.

That lunatic Jim belongs in prison. I could tell you stories." Which his father proceeded to do and they were shocking, if they were true. But Tanner thought they all were probably small town gossip and rumors. He did believe you didn't mess with Jim back then. He must have handled everything from the usual drunks and punks to the biker packs and townie gangs. He had to. You still didn't want to get on his bad side now at fifty-nine. He still had the build, pretty much, of that farm boy who joined the Marines and with his cold black eyes and unruly hair you knew he still played the same game of truth or dare. Sometimes Tanner thought Jim prowled around like he was still in Nam, looking for a fight that he could get his hands on. He found them now and then, as legal as they could be. Tanner had seen him toss around guys like bales of hay. Jim was a shit kicker in his day. They don't make them puny.

Yeah, the old man was a strange one; that was for sure. Tanner brooded as he ducked out of the crowds and cut through the trees. The old man and Jim, now there was a tag team. A duo right out of a Barnum and Bailey dream.

"Shut it down!" Tanner yelled at the kid running the Merry-go-round. The painted ponies were the ultimate danger ride in this wind, at least for toddlers. It could knock them down and break their little crowns and you might not be able to put them back together again.

"Get the kids off! Close the ride! But start it up circling again or the top will blow off!"

"What?"

"Run it with no one on it!"

"I don't get it?"

"Just do it!"

Thunder rocked the reeling rides. Lightning streaked across the blackened sky. The gusts of wind brought bursts of rain. *"Three more!"* Tanner brooded, clothes flapping, hair tossing as he maneuvered through the mobs. The Parachute, the Ferris Wheel, the Spinning Jenny. Fucking Jim. If that crazy old hillbilly was drunk in the back of his van again with some trailer park tramp, Tanner hoped, this time, he got what was coming to him from the old man.

Yeah, Jim sure had his own little harem. Tanner frowned. Tent lights were blinking. Up-ended trash cans were tumbling across the Dream Lanes. The rain lashed at him. A harem for the head honcho – why not when he had plenty of treats to tempt the tricks: popcorn and rides and a wonderland of bright lights and good times. But could Tanner complain? He did plenty of that in his own way. All the ride runners did. His father was right: carnie life would corrupt him.

Dreamland was a dream. Girls were everywhere all summer. Pretty, tanned teasers looking for fun and Tanner was more than willing to oblige them. This was the place to have it. It was in he air like magic. Dream and reality all mixed up, chills and thrills. He had his share of rides through the Tunnel of Love. He had his wild nights, with drinking and gambling and carrying on. But that was on his own time. He wasn't fooling around with bimbos on the job. Tanner was sick and tired of covering for Jim. *"I think I got me a sucker here."* He sure did. All his "volunteers" were. War hero or not, there was a limit. Right now, he wished he were big enough to kick Jim's ass. He deserved it. Look what he was doing to his wife, Beth. 'Course it wasn't his business, but it made Tanner sick. Sanford, Edwards and all them other politicians.

Infidelity seemed to be the law of the land or the craze of the nation. He didn't know if Jim was under the spell of the usual mid/old man life crisis thingamabob or if he had been doing it all along. He sure had been at it since Tanner had known him. Did Beth know what was going on?

She never showed it if she did. Maybe she was just standing by her man. Everybody seemed to stand by her man. Tanner was tired of looking out for Jim and his wild side. Screw the medals.

If it wasn't for Beth, the old man, his volunteers, Jim would probably be a hobo panhandling for cheap wine and change, if his brawling didn't land him in prison. After a couple of years in the military Tanner would muscle up. He imagined himself with big biceps. He would come back and knock Jim's block off, just for the hell of it.

"Shut it down!"

Tanner cupped his hands and hollered at the kid running the Spinning Jenny. Mouths open, eyes wide, laughing, screaming, waving their arms as they flew in all directions, inside out and upside down, the spinners were having the time of their lives, as the wind and rain lashed at them and they whirled around, maybe in some imaginary Katrina or other catastrophic dilemma from which they soon would be rescued safe and sound.

"'Bout time!"

The kid shook his head and hollered back. He was wearing a big popcorn carton on his head as a rain helmet.

"Where's Jim?"

The old man was, suddenly, standing beside him, dressed in a fancy rain slicker with a matching hat – an outfit that must have cost about as much as a Cadillac.

"In the back, last I saw him." Tanner lied. "Some trouble in the arcade. I think a fight."

95

"I can't contact him." The old man stared at his hand radio, which was sputtering and hissing. "All I get is static. We're closing. If you see him tell him. Tornado warnings for almost every town, village and hamlet. Mute point at this point." The old man looked around.

"Everybody's leaving anyway."

The crowds had finally given up on Dreamland for the day and were taking off in droves as the rain came pounding down the Dream Lanes. Some were running, or moving at a trot, trying to beat the mass migration to the parking lot.

"I'll tell him." Tanner looked up over the trees at the Ferris Wheel, which was still circling around with riders, the cars rocking with the gusts of wind. "Soon as I shut down the Parachute and the Ferris Wheel."

"Never mind that." The old man snapped. "Just look for Jim and help him in the arcade or whatever he's doing."

"Fucking Jim!" Tanner cursed to himself as he stalked through the fleeing mobs. He knew where to find him; that was no problem. Jim's beat-up van would be parked, as usual, somewhere in the ring of trees which surrounded the old man's mansion. So what was his detail? Help Jim? *"Hey Jim, move over man. The old man sent me. It's my turn."*

"We're shutting down!" Tanner pounded on the counters of the barker booths as he went along. "Twister's coming. Hide the leaded ducks, the blunt darts and crooked target rifles! Batten down the hatches! Evacuate before it's too late and tell Jim if you see him!"

"Slow down soldier." A grip like iron grabbed him – Jim. "Don't spook the crowds son. They're spooky enough without you announcing cyclones."

A popcorn bucket pulled over his head, sporting his usual shit kickers grin, Jim hovered over him. "So the old man's shutting everything down, even the underground eateries and the Tunnel of Love? Must be a bad one."

"Jim. Where you been?"

Tanner gave him the evil eye, his face grim.

"Puttin' a pony down." Jim shook his head, his expression forlorn. "That new Shetland went wild, threw a kid, buckin' and kickin'. When the runner tried to grab him, he bit him. I chased him off, gave the kid first aid. The kid's OK, just bumps and bruises, scared. We may have a lawsuit on the way. They can't hit the old man for any kind of real money; but the park don't need the bad publicity. It'll probably all get settled in a friendly way, a key to Dreamland, free everything for the rest of the season. I had to call the sheriff, the vet, make a report. Sure did hate putting that pony down. You know how they are, cute as buttons, like little toys. But you can't take chances. He was kicking up a storm, damned near broke my arm." Jim held up his hand and Tanner noticed his arm was wrapped in a sling. "Maybe he was half crazy anyway and the big blow riled him? We'll have to see what the vet says. Hope he wasn't carrying anything contagious."

"Sorry to hear that."

Tanner swallowed hard and felt ashamed.

"All in the day." Jim shrugged and his smile returned. "You got it done, son. I been lookin' around. All the danger rides down. Good job. If you want to stay on the clock, make some extra pay, I got some soft duty to throw your way. I need me a big blow emergency merry-go-round babysitter trainer. Somers is the trainee. Good kid. He's always looking for extra work. Says he needs the money for college. He's there now. Dogs in a steamer and cold brew waitin' for you. A bag of clothes in the office you can change into. Clean jeans, sweatshirts, rain slickers. Pants a little big but you can hitch them up. Be good enough. I'd get him started, myself, but after I close down I got to get back to the stable. Vet's still there. We got to figure out what happened and I still got to bury that pony somewhere. When I'm done I'll drop around."

"No problem." Tanner found himself mumbling. He couldn't face Jim. Not the way he damned and cursed him. He knew how hard killing that pony had been for him. Jim loved those little horses, for some reason. His face lit up every time he looked at them. He was always petting and patting them, giving them sugar cubes, drawling Southern nothings in their twitching ears. "Somers is a cool dude. I'll help him get going."

"You'd be helpin' me too, as usual. Stay as long as you want. All night if you've got nothing to do. The old man will grumble some at having to fork out the extra funds. But training must be done, and if anyone can do it he knows it's you. The old man has noticed you.

He ain't no fool."

"Fucking Jim." Tanner brooded as he cut across the crowds toward the offices. *"He always wins."* He felt guilty and angry at the same time because it could just as well have been the other way with Jim having himself another roll in the hay. Still, it put some pep in his step, Jim's compliments on how well he'd done and the old man knowing who he was.

"Mary, Mary, quite count weary."

In the cinder brick fortress, which looked more like a military installation than an amusement park office, Mary, the old man's daughter, was seated at her desk recording stacks and piles of money down to the penny.

"Tanner, Tanner, mind your manner."

She frowned as she counted. The take had been bad, the day's receipts way off. The old man would hit the roof.

"Penny for your thoughts."

She waved him off.

He found the bag of dry clothes and changed in the washroom. It felt good. He donned the yellow raincoat, pulled up the hood and went out into the monsoon.

"Somers!"

The riderless carousel was circling around in the blackened downpour, lights blazing, calliope music playing, painted horses bobbing up and down.

"Under here!" Somers poked his yellow-hooded head out from the hatch beneath the floorboards. "Studying the gears. Trying to figure out how you shut that damned music off before it drives me nuts!"

"I'll show you how it all works." Tanner crouched down in the whipping winds. "Keep the music on 'til the crowds are gone. You may want to keep it on all night; gets spooky looking at those charging horses going round and round without a sound. Besides, it helps you stay awake. Keep the lights on. Jim keeps a watch from his shack. If he don't see them, he'll think something's happened. There's a tarp under there, a pole and some folding chairs. Bring 'em out and I'll show you how we make a tent. I'm gonna slow it down a bit." Tanner pulled the lever. "Got it going a little too fast."

"Bombs away!"

Somers tossed out the pole. Tanner slid it over and plunged it down a deep small hole. The tarp came next. There was an iron ring wrapped up in it. Tanner fixed the ring on the top of the pole and threw the tarp over it. There were hooks in the ground to which he attached loops at the ends making a little poncho-like tent.

"Looks like a teepee." Somers scrambled out of the hatch carrying the folding chairs.

"More like a headless Mexican bandit to me. Here's the opening. Jim put it together for the merry-go-round babysitter when the park opened. Said he found out about the top blowing off the hard way. The old man told him, with these winds, he should have anticipated that. Jim says he thought the old man was the expert in aerodynamics."

"The ride's that old?"

"Don't look it, does it? But it's the original. Those painted ponies were created by Eastern European craftsmen. Jim says each one should be in a museum."

"I guess they are something, now that I look at them."

Somers watched the carousel horses circle before him, nostrils flaring, manes flying, eyes on fire, legs leaping."

"Let's get in!" Tanner held open the flap for him. A small steamer of hot dogs and a box of beer on ice circled around the carousel. Tanner grabbed them and ducked inside.

"Fucking Jim." He brooded as he sat down next to Somers and dug in. *"You can't stay mad at him."* "When and if the blow stops you can go home. Jim will let you know. I had to stay all night once. Almost drove me nuts. There's nothing to worry about. The ride will keep going.

If anything weird happens, if anything starts to fall apart or starts blowing off, contact Jim. He gave you a hand radio? OK. But if that don't work, if there's too much static, turn off the lights. Jim will be here in a flash."

Tanner liked Somers. They had been in classes together. Somers was smart, cool. They should have hung around with each other more through school.

"Hear you're joining?"

Somers popped his beer.

They ate and watched the carousel, listening to the thunder rumble and the winds wail.

"Looks that way." Tanner shrugged. "Got to get through this recession. After, I'll go to college on the G.I. Bill. Hear you're startin' now?"

"I'm going to give it a shot." Somers frowned as he chewed his hot dog. "Since I have some kind of job. Seasonal, menial, but maybe I can pick up another something for the winter. I'll have to live at home for four years, go to a state school. I applied for a 'needs' scholarship but I doubt if I'll get it. My parents can't help me with anything more than room and board. It's going to be hard, maybe impossible. But I can't complain. Most people I know are just trying to survive these days. Keep a roof over their heads, feed their kids."

"Stars twinkle above."

The calliope music blared amidst the raging storm.

"It's the loveliest night of the year."

"When I was a child, I rode a painted pony on a carousel surrounded by my family, who waved at me, merrily, as I whirled toward my happy destiny, dreamily."

"What's that?"

Somers laughed.

"Nothin'. Just made it up. I'm hoping to be a writer in the future. The teachers always told me I had a knack."

"It's all dreamland ain't it," Somers sighed and sipped his beer, "life?"

"Yeah, 'til you get on a real danger ride."

"What's that?" The little tent was fluttering, rattling on its pole.

"What?"

"Somethin'." Somers parted the canvas, peeked outside. "It's Jim."

They crawled out and steadied each other, as the wind and rain whipped at them. Jim stood swaying on the merry-go-round. His battered van was parked beside it, engine idling.

He was strapping the dead Shetland pony to a carousel horse, tying the two together so they rode, side by side, bobbing up and down with each other, as the ride went round and round. He guzzled from a whisky bottle as he worked.

"What you doin' Jim?"

Tanner scrambled up the platform. Somers chased up after him.

"You boys can go home." Jim was blind drunk, his expression grim. He lashed the Horses' heads together, took another swallow from his bottle and glared at them. "Weren't nothin' wrong with the pony, vet said." His eyes looked dead. "Scared is all. Scared little pony. No need to kill him." He staggered across the platform and moved the lever. The ride went faster. "Ole man wouldn't a kept him no ways. Useless little pony. Too scared. Would of sold him to a glue factory." He downed the rest of his bottle. Pushed the lever further. Tanner and Somers had to hold onto each other. "Tired of killing." Jim muttered. "You boys git."

The ride was reeling, the tent top flapping and fluttering. Tanner and Somers jumped off, just as Jim shut the ride down and the top went flying like some great ghost into the storm.

WAR AND PEACE

He walked the streets,
shook uncontrollably. Couldn't find
a job. Five years after army discharge
we met him in the mission.
We both had been to 'Nam.
We wanted to help the next
generation of veterans. No one was –
the government, the tax system. They were
getting screwed left and right.
No one paid any attention to them.
Other veterans started an organization
"Wounded Warriors –
Say a Prayer For Peace."
Got me and Pete mad. All the money
soldiers had to beg for. They should
of had money to take care of the
soldiers if they want to send them
off to war
Five years, ten years, a little at a time
had made life easier for Jim. With an official
discharge, with a pension coming, the
country boy, whom they talked into
war, would finally have a good life.
Going and coming.
like a skeleton running.
We finally helped him.
He was a sad, frightened
middle-aged man.

TOXIC TOWN

Cabbage soup, cabbage salad,
stuffed cabbage, boiled cabbage,
sauerkraut – everyone in the
tenement ate cabbage everyday,
everyone in the town. You had
to eat something.
You couldn't breathe anyway.
The factories smothered the town
with toxic clouds. Smoke from
their chimneys filled the streets
and alleys. It could have been
London. It could have been Heaven.
Maybe angels flew with the wind.
You couldn't see anything.
My father had a face which looked
like a kicked in door.
My mother had a face which looked
like a cabbage cooker.
It's hard to describe hell well.
I got drafted — three squares a day,
meat, potatoes, pie à la mode.
The air was filled with bullets, explosions.
Couldn't wait to get home.

HOME COMING

A dull gray day, despite the whiteness
of the falling snow, as steeple bells toll.
"Irish Town" is buried in snow. Fierce
flurries off the ocean whorl in with the
north wind – a satin shroud descending.
Ghost ships fill the harbor. Houses huddle
together, like castaways, refugees, shaken
by the stormy weather. I keep to the cover
of the hoardings along the water, a dark,
stiff silhouette of a soldier, down dilapidated
streets, around tumbledown tenements,
past poor men's pubs, shabby storefronts,
many boarded up, posting notices For Rent.
At a gaunt, grim building, I slip in from the
blizzard, cross carefully through a darkened
corridor, quietly climb the staircase. The garret
at the top is stifling and dark, filled with the
odors of the rubbish piled along the landings
of the lower floors by the other tenants.
Warped walls, cracked ceilings, rotting rafters,
stanchions and beams – I lay my duffle bag
at the foot of the bed, hang my army issue coat
and hat in the closet. Despite the fairyland
of falling snow which whirls outside the
garret window, the streets below look bleak,
lonely, hopeless, mean. I had forgotten how
shoddy the houses were along the waterfront,
how hard life had been for the souls who lived
in them, when they lost the American Dream.

REX SEXTON

TAPS

Crawl for cover,
feel death's finger
slide up your spine
as bullets fly and your
buddies die.
Think of your mother,
brother, sister, father,
lover, your Uncle Sam
who got you into this
jam fighting for your life
in Vietnam.
Tell the rosary on the beads
of sweat that run down your
face, neck. Turn a deaf ear
to the moans and groans all
around you that send shocks
through your bones.
Now you are alone, wasting
away in a back street cheap room,
shot to shit at sixty-six from all
the bad habits you picked up in
combat: drugging, boozing,
hiding from the enemy which
came to be reality.
You survived the ambush that
day and many more that came
your way.
But they made you pay.

"DRUMBEATS POUNDING A RHYTHM TO OUR BRAIN"

We lit fires in the woods and danced around
the flames, dressed up like Indians in feathers
and war paint – or nothing at all.
The girls wore bangles, bracelets, beads and
rings. They were painted up too, half-naked and
beautiful.
We drank and smoked dope listening to blasting
rock and roll. We laughed, made love, whooped
and screamed on those summer nights after
high school in what seems in memory like youth's
Mad Dream.
This was long ago and far away in a town I never
saw again after Vietnam. I sometimes wonder
what happened to everyone there with me in the
woods partying like savages, so briefly, before we
became ghosts, widows, orphan-makers, cripples,
or down-and-out writers trying to solve life's riddles.

MANEUVERS

The bus arrives in the city as night comes on,
tunneling off the backstreets to the terminal
underground, which seems packed with every
lost soul the devil could drag down – junkies, winos,
pushers, pimps, beggars, hookers, small time cons,
drifters, runaways, the down-and-out, and huddled,
here and there, in the corners, on the stairs, or sitting
on the floor amidst the sleeping drunks, a number
of homeless families taking refuge from the cold.
I'm in between nowhere and no way out, discharged
after two tours, no prospects, no job, caught in the middle,
of nowhere with time run out.
(Find a mission, scrounge a flop, hit the streets in the
morning, look for some luck?) I shoulder my duffle bag
and maneuver, carefully, through the mob, who crowd
the drafty shadows along the stairway life forgot.
Stateside is just another battle to survive.

AND OVER THE EARTH WHAT?

Rain lashes the troop train and we light 'em if we got
'em, as the broken down leviathan lurches across the
storm pounded stateside wasteland, hauling its monstrous
killing apparatus and the remnants of what is left of us,
while wailing a death-drone like howl of agony, periodically,
as it coils through the jumbled rocks and twisted trees.
"How do you spell amputee?" Ricker looks up from his
letter and asks no one in particular since we're packed
together like smoked sardines. "Like in, 'Barbie you still
fixin' to marry me now that I'm an amputee?'"
"With two ee's." Crawly offers. "Like am pu tee, ee ee."
"Maybe you should just tell her you're a crip, so forget it."
"But add that if she does she'll regret it when they fit you
up to the max with your brand new army issue prosthetics."
"How do you spell prosthetics?"
I feel sick. Train sick. Homesick.
Or maybe I've just
had a belly full of it. We can see nothing. Sheets of rain
blot out the shapes of everything. Veils, shrouds, ghost
swirls tumble past the windows.
"I feel like I'm in a washing machine." Cox complains.
"Don't worry soldier, they gonna hang us all out to dry
when it's over. Who you writin' Slim?"
"God, as usual." I look up and force a grin.
"My, my, HIM!"
Doors in the rain, I scribble on the fly of a book
by Thomas Wolf: "You Can't Go Home Again,"
*locked, lonely, all the same. And the long night
turning into daylight, where we fall through the
cracks like vanishing acts.* I glance at the cramped vets,

try to continue with a stanza that fits.
"I don't like this box a bit! There's no way out of it!"
"You're in a coffin, you idiot!"
Somehow the curse began. The wizard said "Shazam!"
(Or maybe he said: "Be damned?") It was all over
then. We would never be the same again. Snipers, road
bombs, scrambled brains, our wide, staring eyes like the
dead, economic conscripts moving from no jobs, no prospects
into a Holy War that has no end, left with voices that can
no longer be heard, stiff, swinging limbs like lead, feet with
no direction to tread. Was it some "act" that set us back?
Was it the falsification of some fact? How did we end up
on the wrong track with no turning back?
"Barbie would never leave me."
Ricker looks at his letter wistfully.
"Sure not Rick, now that you're so pretty,"

SACRED RITES

Moon shadow was spiritual in the ancient Sioux way.
She spoke to the wind, the moon and the stars.
She married Night Walker on the top of Bear Butte.
It was a ceremony the Sacred Mountain had waited centuries to see.
That night, wild game crackled on spits.
There were drums, dancers, holy chants.
Night Walker was a descendent of Medicine Men.
High chiefs traveled to Pine Ridge from faraway lands.
That was the legend.
Red Leaf drove in a daze.
His head was pounding.
His body pulsed with pain.
Was the Sacred Mountain getting closer?
He squinted through the desert blaze.
If he could make it to the mountain, his soul would return.
The jeep rocked on its wheel rims, bent out of shape.
Broken glass covered the dashboard, floor boards, seats.
His uniform was in shreds. His dog tags choked his neck.
He could walk faster, Red Leaf brooded, as he steered the creeping
jeep, if he were able to walk. He could swim the white rivers, leap
the quick streams, race through the forests, if he still had his legs.
Rainbow trout flew through the air.
Silver water cascaded down golden cliffs, crashing, careening along
tree lined river banks.
Rainbow trout leaping…
A rainbow arched across the sky.
The jeep rattled down the desert road, Red Leaf slumped inside,
until it hit another roadside bomb.

FIGHTING DEMONS

Moving blind, his eye round and dazed,
he looks with rapt bewilderment at the
congregation. There is hatred in his face,
fear, rage. He wants to curse us, kill us.
"Jesus got you brother! Let it go! Let
Jesus take control!" someone shouts.
His mouth looks bluish. It looks like it
might foam. The congregation touches
and fumbles at each other as he pitches
and sways before them. He is testifying.
His lips splutter.
"Evil eye! Watching!" He yells.
"Let him come back Lord!" A woman
entreats. "Your will be done!"
They are called Holy Rollers. They scream,
shout, carry on at their services.
I was five. We were part of their
congregation for a while. My father got
attracted to them. He was a farm boy.
His childhood made him familiar with
revival meetings. He almost seemed
hypnotized as he looked at them.
The war did something to my father. It
wasn't until his death, funeral, military
burial that I found out why – let's just say
he was one hell of a heroic guy taking on
the Japanese bunkered in their caves
with his flame thrower again and again
day after day until they were cleared. He
got that job because he was an ex-athlete,

Depression era boxer, minor league baseball
player, high school basketball star.
Somehow surviving a hell in which most
men would have been felled. To hell and
back.
He would carry on in the middle of the
night – scream, shout, curse like a madman.
He swallowed hard as he watched the
suffering man. The man was wrestling
for his spirit, with demons? The Devil?
Maybe my father was too?
I guess war can do that to you. Hard times
as well.
Life can be Hell. The good can turn evil.
My mother wanted no part of it. The
services terrified my brother and my sister.
That was long ago. Time healed my
father's soul.

We found out about my father's
heroic exploits at his
funeral. From out of
nowhere a military detachment
appeared and took over.
They gave him a 3-volley
gun salute by seven riflemen
after a flurry of military
maneuvers. Speeches were made.
Stories by his colleagues in battle
were told.
Other stories were being rendered
silently.

Hundreds of people from all facets
of society showed up to say farewell
to him – more than any local politician
would ever command.
My father was gentle and honest, very
kind-hearted, caring, always there if
someone needed him.
Perhaps, one of the medicines that soothed
his soul was becoming an expert
horticulturist. We moved from the city
to the suburbs when I was ten.
Our new home had a garage and
a giant backyard. My father
decided to raise flowers. It became a passion.
He transformed that plot of ground into a
garden of earthly delights.
The flowers became a memorial to the
Japanese soldiers he had brutally
killed in the caves. His dahlias,
roses, sunflowers all won trophies
in competition all over Chicago and
its suburbs. He donated these flowers
to hospitals, churches, schools
in the community, along with his services
as a gardener and landscaper.
And so his funeral
became a tribute to him. My father was a
truly remarkable American – one
of the best of his or any other generation
I would imagine.
We had a devastating split over
the Vietnam War. I could not accept it.

In fact, I tried to dodge it. Eventually,
I was drafted and sent to the
Pentagon, assigned to Defense Intelligence,
Given a top secret security clearance,
trained in the complex decoding
of satellite information. I. Q. tests, I guess.
But, I made my father proud in the end.

THE MACHINE

At the factory, Ramon and me would
slit boxes, all night, on treacherous
machines. A run of long oblongs and
then a run of squares, and then the other
way around, then vice versa; to be loaded
on conveyors for the crews down the line
for printing and strapping, to pass on in
stacks to the fork lifts who hauled it all
to the trucks on the docks.
Feeding the slitters and clearing the jams
was the main challenge. The machine
settings were merely simple adjustments.
But fingers could be lost in the operations –
not exactly the job of choice for an aspiring
artist and classical guitarist.
"What you humming, amigo?" I would ask
Ramon. "Is that a new composition, or is
your stomach growling?"
"My stomach was OK, my friend, until I
saw your new painting."
Somehow we managed to get through each
shift without being mutilated, although many
times we were both high on the stimulants
we took to keep us awake, after classes all
day. "Maybe you paint better with no fingers,
my friend? Maybe you don't paint no worse?"
"Your music sounds like machine noise, amigo.
Can't tell the difference."
Ramon got killed in Vietnam. I got drafted as
well; but I was spared the danger of that big

slitter the politicians keep running to maim
and murder each generation, which they
operate so well.

REX SEXTON

THE POLITICIAN

You walk into a room,
study the faces, expressions.
You know right off where
the bodies are buried, the
skeletons hidden. Who's on
the take, who's on the make,
who's selling themselves, or
something, or someone else –
you know all of this. Your
opponents do too.
You fight fire with fire, not
holy water, on Capitol Hill.
Sparrows peck, chickens peck,
eagles swoop and kill, too swift
for detection.
That's how you win an election.

LET THERE BE LIGHT

Cold in my skin, hardened like dead
wax, I sit in the darkness and envision
that soft flame that burned brightly for
everyone, lighting the way in better
days. Sirens wail, lost souls scream,
the gutters run with acid rain. Like a
one note rhythm on a heartbeat drum,
the clock ticks, the pendulum swings,
as throughout the dead zone, each second
the present falls back into the past, while
it falters toward a future, which ends
when it begins, marching in a lockstep
down the calendar of regrets tick by tick.
Everything is gone. There is no reason
to go on. For too many of us, faith, hope,
charity, compassion, liberty, equality,
fraternity, have all died in a country
that lost its dream of decency.

H U M A N K I N D

Our congregation of biological gadgets,
Gyrating through the dynamics of physics.

"FINDERS KEEPERS, LOSERS WEEPERS"

It begins: that first step – I act, therefore, I am.

So do atoms. Do we move or follow them when we use our limbs, engage our brains?

Is it action, reaction, cause and effect that we walk into at birth?

Or are we free to journey through life as we please, as free as a breeze – free agents, spirits, kicking down doors, knocking down barriers, squeezing through cracks, looping though loopholes, driven and directed by our goals, desires, aspirations, from which, if we stick with it, we will ultimately achieve everything we want. Or is it something in between?

Is the way of the brain the same? Are we propelled in set directions by the mechanics of an action, reaction motion contraption assembled and programmed by biological selection to try to meet our needs for survival and procreation? Or is there, in this case, too, something more heroic going on, the machinations of a self-actualized entity and not an automaton? On the other hand, if you were raised by a pack of wolves what would you be? An astrophysicist contemplating the moon and stars instead of howling at them like your hairy brethren.

We awaken gradually from childhood's sleepwalk with some facility to think and talk, at least, as best as each of us is taught. We're not sure yet where or what we are or why we're here or anywhere. That speculation will be filled in eventually, one way or another. Fortunately, we were given a rethink mechanism in our survival kit, some things just don't add up, and we can reexamine the life lessons of our mentors and avoid being brainwashed. Few of us use it. Nevertheless, we can do a redo, weigh and measure and make ourselves over if we deem it necessary, aided by a shrink most likely.

Or is this something of an illusion, too? Is our makeup so complex that we don't notice the subtle tricks of cause and effect, the action, reaction, slights of hand that perhaps shape all our decisions, from without and not within? We face the unknown, look back at the inevitable, they say. Is the smoke and mirrors of our life and times so chimerical that our redo is psychological voodoo?

In the midst of our fairy tale bliss puberty hits. Nothing is uncaused and no one is self-caused and so the heat is on. The drums pound. The fires rage. The hunt is on. The beat goes on, loud and strong, mesmerizing, stupefying. We take its rhythms to our graves. Yet existential progress is made. We learn to reason, reflect, investigate, calculate, meditate despite our breathless tumbles in the jungle. Do these abilities make us the masters of our fates?

We all have experiences beyond our control. The first is birth, the last death. Sexuality is in between and of course there are those pesky taxes the government sticks us with. What other birth defects does life come with? What do we get to pick to put on our birth certificate? Gender? No. Race? No. Nationality? No. IQ? No. Looks? No. Place of birth? No. Neighborhood? Social status? Parents? Siblings? Family tree? Rich man? Poor man? Talents? No. Abilities in math, science, art, music, drama, athletics, etc. like everything else worth having, money and influence especially, have to be inherited, a gift from lucky gene combinations. Education? You can get one if you have the means and we all know what that means. An ivy league school is not in most peoples' scheme of things. That birthday suit sounds more like a straitjacket the more you think about it. Beyond that, life contributes to the lucky or unlucky star list. I lose my job and kill myself. You are in a car crash and die. A lightning bolt sets fire to the theatre and everyone fries. My worst enemy wins the lottery. There is always the unexpected. Although some say that while not everything is predictable everything is, nevertheless, inevitable and if you could record everything that is happening everywhere at any given moment and fed this information into a computer, you could predict the next one and its consequence and so on: how, when, where, why, Frankie killed Johnny, or Sluggo kissed Nancy, or Albert decided to square energy instead of money. What we need is an existential warning system, something like the weather service provides so we can evacuate before the hurricane arrives. We need that in our lives. As free as a breeze? I think they go with the blow, warm or cold, gentle or bold.

This seems to be a cold, mechanistic planet we inhabit, the more you think about it, spinning in a universe indifferent to our wishes, dreams, fears, passions. One that will do what it must with us, as trapped as we are in its dominion of cause and effect and the laws of physics. Causal determinism says that there is an unbroken chain of prior occurrences stretching back to the origins of the universe and that the past and the present dictate the future. In this cosmic confection we are all players on a stage, not authors or directors. The script was written long ago, in one big bang, on which, as the stars burn out, the curtain will ultimately close and humankind is just a conglomeration of biological gadgets gyrating to the dynamics of chemistry and physics. Ouch.

Then there is religion, which is puzzling with its have your cake and eat it too supreme being, an all-powerful entity who created everything and knows all that will happen, right down to every choice, so that one's life must be predestined. Despite this, one somehow must choose good over evil, right over wrong or face hell and damnation and never get to heaven.

We are all trapped in time and place – for many the wrong one at the wrong time all the time. Just visit a slum. Freedom of thought fans, however, like the followers of Ayn Rand, find free will, while an illusive concept, may be less illusory than the determinists make it out to be. Unlike our physical actions, which some say are directed by, and at preordained collisions of atoms in preset locations, making life a process of keeping prefixed appointments, our cerebral life is evanescent. We meditate, ruminate, imagine, ponder, figure, calculate and can come to equally reasoned and convincing, opposite and opposing, conclusions about the same things, like volition and determinism and innumerable other matters, with the confidence that we are not merely positing preordained collisions of our brains' subjective proclivities, since we formed our opinions so carefully and see their rationale so clearly, either this way or that.

The volition proponents are more optimistic, at least on the surface, and don't rely on the god of the machine (Nature) and the ingenuity of its mindless inevitability to settle things. Free Will is having the power of choice in shaping of one's life, in the absence of impediments of course: social, physical, political, psychological, intellectual, monetary, monetary, monetary. Did I leave anything out? In this way of looking at things, there are heroes and villains and prizes handed out for the winners of competitions. Everyone thinks they are going to get one. Really. All one has to do is keep ones' nose to the grindstone, ones' hand to the wheel, ones' eye peeled and never quit until you've gotten it, the rainbow's pot of gold, the brass ring. Whatever, it's a sure thing.

Now we're ready for that first step! So, step right up! Go for it! Place your bet, tot! Everyone can win! It isn't in the stars! It isn't in the cards! Your life is in your hands! No matter who you are, rich or poor, humble or grand, smart or challenged! You can make it! Yes, you can!

You say the game sounds rigged to you, the dice loaded, the casino crooked? You say some get favored and most get gypped when things are handed out, and few, if any, could have built or earned whatever they have without those gifts of fate or luck. And you think it's a pity that the mechanism cranking out our story has so little humanity, so much suffering and misery for which there is no necessity? You wonder why the script can't be changed, the gears of the cosmic machine rearranged, at least on our small planet by social dynamics to make life balanced and fair so everyone can live a little better? You say you want more?

More! Well at least you said "please sir" but look you little beggar, life is unfair! That's why we're having this talk! Finders Keepers, Losers Weepers! Now suck it up! Get out there, you little whiner! Beat those odds!

KAFKA

The treatments that keep me alive also destroy
my immune system – death on the installment
plan or death as a catch can? I guess that's
the plan.
Consequently, I'm in the hospital regularly
with pneumonia or some other kind of medical
malady. This last time was for a mystery
infection. They never did find it. They got
it to go away by bombarding me with so many
drugs they also blew my addled brains away.
In the midst of that they decided to perform a
lung procedure on me. If it worked, my immune
system killing treatments could lessen and
maybe I'd get sick less often. It was risky
though. I had to sign a lot of forms stating
that if they killed me in the process it was
okey dokey.
The procedure went badly. I woke up, sort of,
in the middle of the night in Intensive Care.
Not that I knew where I was, who I was, or
anything for that matter.
I had something stuffed down my throat.
I grabbed it and pulled and pulled. It was
a breathing tube. Don't try this at home
kids. It's extremely dangerous. I learned
the next day that no one had ever ripped out
their breathing tube. It's more complicated
than you think. It's a miracle that I didn't
cause permanent damage to my trachea or
rip something and drown in blood.

The next day the doctor asked what happened.
I said: "I don't know. Suddenly everything
got Kafka-esque."
She stared at me blankly.
I said: "Do you know who Kafka is?"
She said: "No."
Kafka, the guy who stands for the dark side
of existence. How about Orwellian?
Dickensenian? Shakespearean? Any, all, of
the giants of literature who define our
deepest most profound thoughts and feelings.
Do these techo wizards really know these
human emotions. Should I really sign my okey
dokey over to them?

The soul is a prism
That casts rainbows
From heaven

CHINA MOON

Artists live where all dreams end. Truth,
Illusion are a dance of apparitions. You
try to capture them. Smoke and mirrors are
what you usually get – but sometimes life's
magic. The blackened windows of the
Chinatown streets are filled with plucked
ducks hanging by their necks. Philly has
seen better days. So, has every city in the
USA. Fortune Cookie Avenue ran out of
lucky sayings.
Homeless in doorways, or asleep in alleys,
huddled under cardboard, or shivering in
the moonbeams … as dreams of glass
shatter across the shimmering cities, making
towers tremble and angels tumble like the
ashes from a modern Dante's Inferno.
The moon is American: our baseball in the
heavens. But the game has been lost, the
stadium in pandemonium.
In my rundown tenement, where empty
pockets don't feed the family or pay the
rent, we all wait for some miracle which
is heaven sent. One bad day we all say.
Tomorrow will bring another one.
They go on and on.
Five flights of steps to my ghetto garret,
where I can see the moon round and bright,

tonight, above the urban blight, shining
like a tower guard's spotlight on the
prisoners below, huddled in their hovels,
or tossing in the shadows, or cooking
scraps for their families on leaky gas
stoves. A China moon to inspire me to
paint the magic of humanity, somewhere
down there, hidden in the misery.

There is a place and time
where your hour is ready.
It is your moment of truth,
your enlightenment, epiphany.

BODY AND SOUL

He woke up alive each day
barely. Each day there was
hell to pay, as cancer ate away his
brain, spirit physical and emotional
stamina. Replaced it
with pain, trauma.
Rattlesnake kills with a single bite.
The rattlesnake bites with all
its might.
The rattlesnake bit into Conti's face.
His head was on fire. Pneumonia
again. A major setback. He would have
to get treated for that first.
It was becoming more hopeless.
It was time to write his epitath.
He would be dead in a few months.
He had a new book coming out with stories
and poems.
All his books were given generous
praise.
Conti was compared to
the great writers in world history.
Coleridge, Kafka, William
Blake. That had been the goal
of his life. To walk that
glory road of literature.
No one reads anymore. The grand
quest for meaning and understanding was
dead. Conti would put on the headstone of his grave:
"Life's weary wander, a white road lost."

THROUGH THE LOOKING GLASS

I dine with Nobel laureates,
Drink with mobsters.
I came up hard as diamonds,
unpolished and uncut.
I read books, people, paintings, palms.
My wife is a scientist,
white mice calypso in her laboratory,
minerals mambo.
I learned how to paint from a Holocaust Jew,
his specialty was rainbows.
My fiction is dark, violent, mesmerizing.
God is dead.
Literature is dead.
The age of art is over.
I'm told.
Sister Wendy is my patron saint.
She has a picture and a poem of mine
tucked away in her cloister.
I paint fate:
dolls who dream, marionettes who emote,
toys and puppets with hearts and souls.
I paint what I see, tell what I know.

*"When Rex was 18 he died, momentarily. He left
his body and traveled to another dimension. This
experience changed his life. Mr. Sexton paints
another kind of reality."*

Mac Gilman Gilman/Gruen Gallery

What is reality?

145

REX SEXTON

ELEGY

Talk about nowhere, I was there.
We lived in a bungalow on No Man's Road,
near the intersection of Dead End Drive
and Take A Hike Turnpike, in a well=
populated village with few living inhabitants,
where "you'll never take us alive," was the
welcome mat for most of the residents
(along with "don't wake up the dead, we
need them for our overhead") and the only
industries, before they opened the small factory
where my father finally got himself a job, were
the innumerable cemeteries to which caravans
arrived, periodically, to deposit their loved ones
in the lonely, willowy, burial facilities.
I was ten. Both my parents were working then.
My mother commuted to her office job in the city.
My father put in long hours at the factory. They
signed their "rest in peace lease" and buried
themselves alive to pay the bills and raise their
offspring, me.
School was out. I was alone. There were young
couples about with babies in the other bungalows.
No kids my age.
Mists, fog, eerie lights, howls, moans filled the
days and nights. I roamed the graveyards. They
were my home away from home. My friends became
the names chiseled into the weathered headstones.
Everyday was a dream of Halloween. Every night,
in sleep, the departed would creep from their tombs,

vaults, mossy mausoleums, graves and visit me.
Life, death, the mystery of being, joy, sorrow, and
everything in between came with them as stories
written on the wind between the birth and death dates
and transferred to my imagination. Before I knew it,
I became a poet – talk about nowhere.

DEVILS AND ANGELS

Curls of color crowd my work in progress.
They look like tear drops or rain drops or
the outlines of alarm clocks.
I squiggled one on the canvas and then kept
them going, for no reason I can fathom.
Maybe they are a code which holds
the DNA for the painting I am attempting?
A race with time? A nursery rhyme? An
ode to the sublime?
I stare at them through the smoke from my
breakfast of champions.
What's next? Where am I going with this?
In this strange bedlam we inhabit, wedged
in between monkey and human (and being
stoned in addition) anything can happen in
my imagination.
I remember the story Henry Miller wrote
about the angel he painted when he was
loaded. I never painted an angel. Maybe
I'll find one hiding in my canvas when I
connect the dots or tear drops or alarm clocks,
whatever is curled up?
An angel today, a devil tomorrow, nothing
unusual for an artist's studio.
This is the sort of place one comes to ponder
good and evil and to confront that meeting
between thought and instinct, peace and
violence, greed and giving, which we all
share if we dare.

ALL THE PRETTY BALLERINAS

Night's lost wander,
amidst phantoms you'd flee in dream,
through ghost haunts, spectral walks,
dead zones fogged by smoke and gin.
Uptown, downtown, round and round,
falling down...as they dance in black dresses
around the rim of each drink,
the daughters of darkness
who circle the brink.

"She's beautiful."
"She isn't done."
"Who's the model?"
"Death."
"You're crazy! Hey, I know that girl!
She's that ballerina, your old flame.
How come you never paint me?"
"I only paint what I hate."
"You do not."
"War, plague, famine, betrayal –
 I'll paint you, call it 'Midnight Angel.'"
"Where are you going?"
I move from the couch to the easel,
take a hair of the dog on the way,
squint as the sunlight sets the canvas
ablaze. Fat Cats, the Jet Set, the artsy
social whirl, play in my memories of the
pretty ballerina, along with some specter
of myself, who quickly became an
inconvenient oddity amidst that rarefied

swirl with my hard scrabble sketches
of working class life, battlefield drawings,
paintings of the down and out.
"Why are you doing that?"
I ghost the goddess with a solvent-soaked
rag, fade her beauty, erase her eyes.

ART IN THE DARK

Black humor, the dark side of life.
My art is filled with it.
Why the Kafka-esque?
The human condition seems to
ask for it. Somehow what is bad or not
rarely connects. Look at our dysfunctional
families, marriages, politics.
Look at my health. I never took
care of it. There is a mix
of beauty and hopelessness, in what
I accomplish. Longing and regret.
People like their art more optimistic.
I think mine is more accurate.

STERILITY KNOCKS

Writer's block
Maybe I can shoot my
way out of this with the
help of God and a couple
of cops?
Do some noir piece from
my old neighborhood
like the car we stole
when we were teens.
"You look like something
the cat dragged in!" my
wife glared at me.
"Writer's block."
"I heard."
"If wishes were horses
the beggars would ride for free."
"Or take the subway."
"Give it a kick or a kiss,
a lick and a promise."
"What about the cops?"
"You serve time?"
"Not for that one."
"It's so easy to pull the
wool over their eyes."
It's all poets do anyway.
with everyone.
"Give it a try."
My wife don't give
up. It's do or die.

THE GIFT

So this guy, God, hands me a claim
ticket for a box with nothing in it.
"Enjoy."
He yawned and life went on.
"What kind of gift is this?"
I asked my parents, as if they
might know or even think about it.
"It's a whatchamacallit."
My father said staring at the TV.
"Go ask the Rabbi."
My mother frowned and glared at me.
"What am I supposed to do with this
empty box?" I asked the Rabbi.
"Put something in it?"
He shrugged and scratched his head.
Profound, I thought. I hustled and
bustled and tried to fill it up.
By the time I got old the box was
as empty as when I began, the way
the stuff of life came and went.
I used it for my coffin.

REX SEXTON

ACCIDENTAL TOURIST

Visiting the Holocaust museum in D.C.
really wrecked me – a black hole of human
nature that sucked me into a nightmare.
I fled to the National Gallery where wild
flowers and butterflies dance on walls under
sunny skies – Calder, Matisse, those bright
colors and shapes making a harmonious
symphony of reality. Some artists can take you
to La La Land, where life is beautiful and living
is grand. I'm not sure where they're coming
from. No place I've been. But more power
to them. We definitely need them.

SOME PEOPLE

Death grins confront Goodie as she enters the freezing lobby,
shivering in her paper-thin, museum security uniform,
while sensors sound alarms around the marble ghosts
of Greek and Roman gods.
"Goodie to Control."
Goodie chatters into her hand radio.
"Go for Control Goodie."
"Why is Satan smiling in my face all over the place?
You best get some broom boy over here
to knock these devils down and that squawk is the Hawk
some fool let in." *Damned fools!* Goodie grumbles
as she looks around the screaming room. The glass wall
of windowed doors is a glaze of ice, showing silhouettes
of stiletto-death from icicles dangling across the entrance ledge.
That night shift ain't worth shit! Goodie all but spits.
*Must of left them doors wide open again when they delivered
the flowers for that Million Dollar Donor wing-ding.*
Goodie digs into the lobby cabinets, huffing and puffing and
cursing to herself, as she pulls out stacks of flyers, art cards,
schedules, museum maps and lays them atop the information desk,
pain shooting down her stiffened back.
"Goodie to Control. Would you kindly call the docents lounge
and remind the ladies school groups comin' soon?"
*Damned docents! taking they own sweet time every day
sippin' coffee while I runs around and gets stuck helpin' them kids
like I ain't got my own job!*
The sensor wails suddenly stop, and with the silence
Goodie hears someone banging on a foggy entrance door.
Good god! Goodie shuffles from the desk to the podium
and grabs her ring of keys. *Museum don't open for another hour!*

155

Says so right on the sign, ceptin' for school groups,
can't someone read!
"I'm coming!" Goodie shouts, as she shuffles across the room.
"Hold on!" But the frosted phantom keeps banging and hollering
and beating the hazed, glass door.
"Praise the Lord!" An angry woman, bundled in furs, bustles past
Goodie and glares at her. "You finally let me in! It seems some
people are a little pokey around here!"
"Maybe some people got arthritis!" Goodie flares.
"Then maybe some people should retire!"
"Maybe some people can't!"
"Then maybe some people should be made to! I'm here for the
donors' breakfast. Don't turn your back on me!"
"Some people got to work, sweetie. That breakfast ain't for an hour.
They be settin' up the coffee soon downstairs."
"'SWEETIE'! Some people are obnoxious! Some people are rude!
Some people don't belong in a Museum!"

AMERICAN GOTHIC

She woke in the cold coughing,
listened to her children
wheezing in the dark.
The angel of death,
beat its black wings
in her fever dreams.
Rain pounded the tenement roof.
"Lift me Jesus."
Floree clenched her calloused fists,
shivering on the sweat soaked bed.
"Lift me lift me Jesus."

Like holy ghosts,
the snow white spirits
slept in the sunlit court,
hushed, celestial, chimeras
carved from clouds of stone.
"Don't touch please."
Floree drifted in a daze,
between the paintings and the statues,
amidst the throngs of milling patrons,
across the chapel-like exhibit room,
feverish in her museum uniform.
"No flash cameras 'mam."

The marble hall seemed
a mist of make believe,
phantoms shifting in a haze.
The statues looked spectral,
even more haunting than usual:

157

Abraham Lincoln, the shackled
man-slave, the Abolitionist woman,
the frail, fragile goddess of truth.
"But I gots to go to work baby."
Floree remembered the morning like
a dream. *"If 'en I don't I don't get no pay*
sweetie. Sides, they makes you get a doctor's
excuse. We ain't got no money for that.
Don't be scared, child. I knows you and Libby
real sick. Misus Gracie gonna look in on you.
I loves you sweetie. I be home real soon."

WITHOUT REALLY TRYING

Sitting alone in this café,
scribbling on bits of pocket
crumpled paper, I notice that
people have a tendency to look
at me, sneakily – men, women,
young and old all poking at little
hand held gizmos, iPhones, Black-
berries, god knows what.
What they seem to see is a mystery.
Someone that does not quite fit into
the reality of their uniformity and
what that should be. While they don't
want to offend, they must peek at "it"
again. I think that I engender this by
simply being a something that is,
obviously, not becoming anything
other than nothing. I don't have that
"How To" book look as they do:
"Succeed," "Attract," "Fix This,"
"Solve That." I guess there's
nothing to be done but grab a fresh
Starbucks napkin and write another
poem.

WRITER'S NOTES

Four drab walls with smog in the window…
dark streets below no one dares to walk through…
creaky bed, small table with a wobble… there's
a hotplate on the window sill.
The bathroom is down the hall. There's a public
phone down it, too, although you never get a call.
The radio on the dresser was purchased from a thrift
shop. The classical music you play on it always sounds
a little shocked.
A shoebox filled with rejection slips lies on the floor
of the closet. Next to it is a stack of literary magazines
with funky names. Each one has a sample of
your work in it – which makes it all worth it.

CAST TO THE WIND

Knives, handguns, handling them
was fun. Not the idea of killing
with them, which we tried hard to avoid.
We grew up in a tough factory town.
We were surrounded by Chicago.
The Chi-town gangs would come at us from every
direction. We fought them to a stand
still, measure for measure, over drugs,
hock shops to handle stolen goods,
competitive heists.
OK'd by gangsters for a cut.
We'd flash ourselves on the streets
each day showing the Chi-town
gangs we were ready for anything.
We'd take them on, never back
down. Many of us stayed
that way. Life often gave us
hell to pay. We did it with
pleasure and in spades.
I graduated from the school of hard knocks,
which informed my vision of
empathy for those whom fate dealt a bad hand.
A punk transformed into a dedicated
and triumphant author. I did it so
I could go to the grave in my poet's remains.

A TAIL OF TWO KITTIES

"Out there, beware, lost souls everywhere, misery, poverty, murder, robbery." The Fat Cat said to Stray who happened to pass his way. "In here, good cheer," he gestured toward the high, arched door he was about to enter, "nothing to fear, nothing to long for, comfort, camaraderie, peace and prosperity. The way life should be."
He tipped his top hat and wished Stray a good day, not without irony.
A doorman bowed to Fat Cat, ushered him inside, and went back
to guarding the entrance again.
Gender? No. Race? No. Nationality? No. Country? No.
Neighborhood? Social status? Heritage? Family tree? Parentage?
Siblings, anybody good for anything? No, no, and no again!
"Curiosity killed the cat. So what!" Stray thought. He was half-dead anyway. He sat "out there" in a seedy bar and made a list of what he was responsible for in his life and what he missed when things were handed out by God or Fate or the Force. Whomever dealt the cards and got him into his mess.
"Looks? No. IQ? No. Talents? Math, science, art, music, athletics, no – like everything else worth having, money and influence especially, talent had to be inherited, a gift from lucky gene combinations. Education? Sure, Harvard or Yale. Ha! Lucky he didn't end up in reform school. Not much came with that birth certificate. Stray brooded. And then you died at the end of it! Stray felt gypped, cheated. He was a patsy. Why was he handed the short end of the stick in everything? Why was he just another mangy alley cat, and an unlucky black one at that, yowling in the darkness? It wasn't fair. He was just a work'us. When he could find work. While these whosits were blessed!
"The fat cats feed off the nation"
Stray scribbled on his bar napkin.
"The strays their hope for salvation.
The hip on jubilation." He continued.

162

"The cool on calculation.

It's a dog's life."

He finished. Hey! He did have some talent! Stray reread the poem he had just written. Not bad. He was a poet and didn't know it. A lot of good that would do him. Just another useless occupation. Thank you Lord, Stray sighed, once again for nothing!

POETS GONE WILD

I press play, palms sweating, hand trembling
and suck in one last gasp of oxygen as Poets Gone Wild
explodes, in full blazing color, on my television screen.
The camera pans a drop dead pandemonium of hip, hot,
happening wordsmiths, all mobbed, in rows, of book browsing
bedlam, between the shelves of a swinging library. Hellbound
Haikuists, Sultry Sonneteers, Tripping Traditionalists, Badass
Beats, Down and Dirty Lyricalists, Proseiacs, Tankkears, Nit and
Gritters, let it all hang out, with bespeckled bravura, as they recite,
declaim and wave lethal chapbooks at the boob tube's screen.
The camera zooms in on the shows M.C., Randy Rhyme.
Rakishly retro in his tweed suit, bow tie, battered loafers,
Randy gazes provocatively at the leering viewer with a
"let's do it" expression on his professorial face.
Beside him, in the close up, is the buxom, bun-haired,
brainstorming beauty, Avan Tguarde. Avan's onyx eyes
sparkle, behind her coke bottle glasses. Her conjugation
grinding teeth, glisten with a secretive smile. She is coyly
caressing a copy of her latest renegade rhetoric, Totally
Blank Verse. Taunting the turned on audience, her ink pen
red fingernails precociously play a game of peek-a-boo with
the creamy pages, parting them slightly and then squeezing
them shut. It is like a tense, tantalizing fan dance from the
risqué poetess, wanton, salacious. Will she? Won't she?
At a wink from Randy, Avan folds the vexing volume she's
been fondling and tucks its spine between her voluptuous breasts.
Heart pounding, breath heaving, face flushed, I grip the arms of
my living room chair, feeling like the lost mountaineer, who,
gasping for air, is miraculously thrust, by a force of nature, into the
summit's aperture, cradled safely in the valley between its majestic

peaks. (But knowing the impending storm is treacherously near.) Suddenly, shockingly, Avan throws back her head and, with an expression of erotic euphoria on her librarian's face, brazenly yanks open the teasing book and exposes the naked pages of Totally Blank ... "Spread 'em baby!" Someone shouts.

All hell breaks loose. The poets go wild. They push, shove, pummel their way, from every direction, into the camera's eye, spreading their pages, exposing their rhymes, brandishing their chapbooks in a brash and bawdy bookworm's bacchanal. A fight breaks out. The battling bards commence to bashing one another about the head (giving new meaning to the expression Slam). Spectacles fly, books are flung, pen duels develop (giving new meaning to the term penmanship). All at once, shelves are raided. A food for thought fight erupts. As volumes are hurled, the camera backs away from a free-for-all which rivals the famous scene from Animal House.

I fall back in my chair in a faint.

NIGHT WITHOUT STARS

Listening to it in the darkness,
the lullaby of hopelessness,
played by staccato rain
across the Chi-town tenements,
gunfire and sirens tossed in
to make the rhythms of the night
even more disturbing,
I dream colors,
paint prayers,
across the blackboard of oblivion,
where all lessons of the street are learned,
without degrees,
and tattooed in the heart and mind
with graffiti signs.

NIGHT SWEATS

The scary lair of sleep
where white mice in lab smocks
dance around alarm clocks.
I am moving, not moving,
somehow being transported,
a step at a time,
around the broken chairs and tables,
between the crushed beer cans and empty bottles,
passed the pile of unpaid rent bills,
toward the easel in my garret corner.
The sky-lit loft is an aquarium of starlight.
Munch-like moons haunt the heavens.
Van Gogh constellations swirl the sky.
Atop the nightstand, paint jars sparkle like prisms.
The ghost-white canvas shines with astral light.
I am painting, not painting.
Slanting forward, I slash the canvas
with road signs, religious symbols, astrological charts,
corporate logos, chemical formulas, designer labels,
mathematical equations, secret signals ...
The creatures from my cracked world, cautiously, climb out
from their demimonde tableaus – their Brut Art rendered gin
mills, strip joints, dice dens, night clubs, jail cells, missions,
soup kitchens, backstreet labyrinths, blind alley flops – bag
ladies, homeless families, penniless pensioners, beggars, winos,
hookers, junkies, grifters, gangsters, orphans, runaways – my
non-sellable oeuvre of the near-dead, and the might-as-well-be
– which includes my sallow "Self Portrait In Straight Jacket,"
rusty dope needles sticking through my head ... They slither down
the warped walls, crawl out from the festering stacks, crowd around

167

me with their dead end eyes, watch me as I work.
I repaint us all in a castle in the clouds, feasting around a royal
table, dressed in finery, flush with merriment, while cherubs circle
chandeliers, and virgins dance on marble floors, and rainbows arch
across a kingdom where ketchup is no longer a vegetable to politicians,
and lives are no longer negotiable to corporations, and liberty, equality,
fraternity reign forever, and no child is left behind.

Anything is possible when nothing is real.

NIGHT WATCH

Out of the black,
star-domed unknown,
nothingness rushes in with a scream,
a shrieking, circular, no more,
which mangles the jungle night with flames.

Vietnam and napalm,
fear death agony destruction
and all for nothing!

Slanting forward, I slash the canvas
with colliding colors, fractured planes,
splintered perspectives, blood-red rhythms,
writhing soldiers, twisted trees,
(gray hair soaked with sweat,
old clothes splattered with paint)
a crazy conflagration of distorted shapes,
which looks like nothing so much
as a Hieronymus Bosch on hash,
(or maybe some asylum inmate's "art therapy" piece)
destined, when it's done, for an exhibit at the
Vietnam Veterans Museum, thinking of Iraq
as I lash away and of the roadside-bombed soldiers,
I read about everyday, reassigned to graves …

"Art tells us the truth about being human."

I remember reading in one of my art criticism books.

So does a bullet.

FAIRY TALES CAN COME TRUE, IT CAN HAPPEN TO YOU

Snow White in a glass casket was what I had been
aiming at with my Surrealistic portrait of the Dead
Zone's crack racket, trying to symbolize the lost soul
in the black hole of the ghetto, and the living-death-
quest of hopelessness all around us. But the chaos
of contours I created in the fairytale beauty's features,
after I started drinking and slashing paint on the canvas,
and the undulating rhythms of brush strokes with which
I concocted her coffin had her come out of my backstreet
fable as an angel wearing a death mask of sable, asleep
on a billiard table. So maybe "Dust" was the thrust of
my journey into oblivion in a game you can't win because
a drug is a drug and there's plenty of "Dust" in the hood.
Besides, while Picasso said that what one paints is what
counts and not what one intended to accomplish, he also
said that if you know exactly what you're going to do
there's no point in going through it. Life lives as it does,
I guess. I'm no Picasso, let's face it; but neither are you.
Dead of winter, I look out at the falling snow from the
window of my ghetto studio. Ragged figures roam the
streets below, dragging through the drifts – bag ladies,
homeless families, dead-enders, penniless pensioners.
And more each day, as the cubical people lose their
lives in the sitcom world and join us in hell: shivering,
pale-faced strangers who come and go, the likes of
which none of us has seen before. As the Dead Zone

grows, wedding rings, good luck charms, Rolex watches
fill the pawnshop windows.
I grab my sketch pad, draw an old wrought iron oven.
On the top of it I put a kettle. Inside I sketch the
portraits of Hansel and Gretel.

REX SEXTON

AMERICAN PIE

Better to blackout than be;
better the bottom of the bottle
than reality – dead end days,
sleepless nights. Why paint,
why write: about the old
lady in the alley asleep in a
doorway, the raggedy kids
playing in the gutter, their
families living in squalor,
the derelicts, lunatics, pimps,
pushers, muggers, killers,
the lost vet begging for cigarettes?
Scenes too real to find a refuge
in bookstores or museums,
amidst the soup cans and
American flags, and the golden
words penned for the aesthetic
ruminations of future generations.

LINE, FORM, COLOR

I stare. I see it emerging
on the canvas, hand and eye
mesmerized by the nightmare
in the room's glare coming to
life.
It is cold in the studio.
Sirens wail outside the windows.
I shiver at the easel.
Gunfire crackles across the ghetto
like insurgent fire in a war zone.
Back and forth, left to right –
faces filled with fear, despair,
hopelessness, along midnight streets
no one would dare to enter unless they
had to because they lived there.
I put away my brushes, paint tubes,
turn out the lights. Enough truth and
beauty for one night.

N O   E X I T

Spider's silk, the thread that weaves
love's web ... we hurdle into it, our
bodies simulating flight as it shimmers
before us in the sunlight, moonlight,
day and night.
Maybe we pray, as we alight, that we
will survive the glimmering net of magic
or regret in which we became entrapped?
Moonlight through the window of
an artist's garret in a ghetto long ago ...
I still see you in that glow, posed like
the statue of an angel forged in first
love's crucible.

DARK DWELLINGS

with windows to the streets.
Dark women in summer shadows,
beautiful women from European
countries: the mothers of my new
classmates and friends.
I recall their look, walk, the
solemn way they dealt with
each day — life in America.
They seemed sad to me at sixteen.
Life is not as spiritual here as it
was there with its museums,
cathedrals, galleries, artists, and
writers.
The husbands were happy, so were
their daughters and sons. The land
of plenty, America rocked with fun.
In high school I was a student
painter. I had published a few
poems in our local newspaper.
Intimacies developed, became
affairs. The dark, beautiful women
and the artistic teen
sharing their lonely
thoughts and dreams.

MY STORIES

I read and wonder,
organize words until
stories emerge.
I don't dream often.
I dream-think.
That's how the writing
gets done.
What is that like?
Something close to hallucination.

"CHOP SUEY"

Blocks of shadows filled the walk-up's grimy windows – boarded-up buildings, rundown tenements, burnt out shells with signs that said condemned. Like what around there wasn't? The city could hang the same signs around his and Rachael's lives, Malcolm reflected, as he sat in the gloomy corner he or his fate had painted them into and pondered his life's disorder. It was a wonder the city hadn't. Two empty rooms heated by death rattle radiators, which hissed at them like vipers, a mattress in the main one was their best effort at furniture, along with a couple of lamps, sans end tables or nightstands. The idle gas stove and the empty refrigerator were courtesy of the slum lord's building manager. The alarm clock, which they never set, was purchased from a thrift shop in the time they were optimistic, along with the static-y Goodwill radio. The classical music Malcolm played on it always sounded a little shocked, as if it couldn't quite adjust to the puzzling change in stations the current owner had made switching from talk radio and hard rock.

Each day ended as soon as they woke up, nothing to do, nowhere to go, no money to spend. Was there a point to even living them? The second room they used for their "artists' studio." That one had track lighting in it, as well as two easels with folding chairs before them, which could have remained folded for the amount of time either of them used them. As for time, there was nothing but time. They were rich in that, and art supplies, tons of it jammed into the closet, canvas, paint, brushes. Somewhere along the way, however, their spirits died. Neither of them felt inspired. Why would they? They were wretched and starving. The usual artist's condition? Maybe back in the day. Neither he nor Rachael could quite get into slum life and poverty.

Feeling cold in his skin, like hardened wax, Malcolm sat in the studio's bright glare and envisioned that soft inner flame that should burn brightly for everyone, lighting the way as it had in better days when hope sprang eternal and anything was possible.

Outside, sirens wailed, lost souls screamed, the gutters ran with acid rain. Like a one note rhythm on a heartbeat drum, the cosmic clock ticked, the pendulum swung, as throughout the dead zone, each second the present fell back into the past, while it faltered toward a future, which ended before it began, marching in a lockstep down the calendar of regrets, tick by tick.

In black space the world sleeps, dreams, spins, holds its center together with stars made of sugar. Malcolm mused as he began to prepare his canvas, a rare occurrence of creative industriousness, driven by desperation more than inspiration and would probably turn out a mess. The cosmic clock ticks for astronauts. The subway rumbles through tunnels that whisper secrets no one can decipher. We paint our lives on air, naïve artists astounded by the miracle of being here. Love is the only color we remember.

"An Artist's Redundant Rendition of Our Curious Congregation of Biological Gadgets Gyrating Uncontrollably to the Dynamics of Physics." Malcolm gave a working title to his effort in progress. Apply gesso, he mused, convoluted convulsions of color follow, as fierce bursts of chaos spin into a madness, which is ultimately harnessed by bold brush strokes that are random and meaningless. Not exactly art school procedures but they worked for Malcolm and form follows function – his being to paint what he felt and not what he saw because that rarely revealed anything at all. Poetry in color was what he was after.

In the painting an imaginary man looks up at a clock. "It must be time to stop." He seems to be thinking, the way his jutting jaw drops.

An imaginary woman walks up to him. Does the rest of what happens ever begin?

A crystal ball is a mystical jewel.

Time is a tool.

Parts make a whole and day after day one part fits into another as the future is made.

There is an imaginary moon above them, in a make-believe night. While none of it is real, all of it is delight.

At least, that is the intention. Malcolm pondered his emerging creation. Maybe his art dealer could sell this one? It certainly was more pretty than profound. Maybe it would match someone's drapes? Put a smile on some socialite's face? He would get a second opinion when Rachael came home. He would sound her out about it. "What do you make of it?" He could hear her now, envision her standing there, scraggly, scrawny, shrouded in hip length tangled black hair, dark eyes flaring, sourpuss glaring. "It's a piece of shit. Paint over it." Rachael the purist. Rachael had disappeared in the morning for parts unknown. Probably looking for a job, which he also should be doing instead of wasting his time with this Romantic concoction.

What Malcolm should be painting, he knew, was the scene that he was facing – the blocks of sorrow looming in his window. He could create a giant, cubist American stalag conundrum with Munch-like phantoms screaming in the windows, Grosz-like Gestapo figures skulking in the shadows, lost souls howling down the avenues. Spinach for the eyes to feast upon which few would care to swallow down. Ah, the artist's dilemma: greeting cards or human graveyards? Reality? Or yet another "eye candy" collector's day dream?

Food for thought was always dessert in the commercial galleries. Angel food cake was the staple of the yuppie collector's diet. Bestseller books, blockbuster movies, toe tapping or hip gyrating tunes, who wanted something to ponder?

There was a way to get around this problem, for Malcolm and any artist. Kink up your concoction. Serve some Devil's food cake. "Black" or "White" were your options in the art world if you wanted to sell. That's how Malcolm got his little bit of artistic recognition in the first place, two years ago in his last year of art school. In a way, his fifteen minutes of fame had come about by accident. Not that he hadn't seized the moment. He had been making sketches of this street singer the neighborhood he was living in called Star, a teenage runaway who sang for her supper on a street corner. She was beautiful, tragic, an angel in a nightmare, as Malcolm saw it. She sang like a lark. It had been his passion as a student to paint her portrait. They worked it out. If he sold the picture he would pay her half of what he got. But it wasn't about the money. He was deeply inspired by the sad, hopeless beauty.

The police found her body in an alley one night, raped and strangled, probably grabbed from behind while she was shivering in the cold waiting to perform, thrown to the ground, punched repeatedly until she was knocked out, dragged back into the shadows, strangled when she came to and fought her assailant. A picture of her ravaged body quickly appeared in the tabloids. Soon after, the story aired on the local news. The gruesome pictures, were also being flashed across the internet. The Sun Times and the Tribune followed. Malcolm saw his chance. Collectors really dug that sort of snarky "street-life meets art" connection. He knew it was smary. He knew he was tarnishing his integrity. But he was fresh out of school and he was hungry for recognition and, okay, fame and fortune. Richter made a bundle off the nurses' portraits he cranked out from the pictures he duplicated from the papers after the Richard Speck slaughter – and they were only knockoffs after the fact, not the real McCoy of an unsuspecting victim smiling and singing as though life was worth living, like he had stashed in his portfolio. Didn't hurt Richter's career either. Nothing could do that. If anything, it enhanced it. And look how Serrano cleaned up with his gory morgue photos. Malcolm could do a series of two-panel before and after concoctions of Star, get the after from the internet or papers. At first, he struggled with the notion. It was the worst kind of exploitation. But not for long. He didn't have long. When something went viral you had to get in on the action. If you passed it up, you could blow your chance. That chance might never come again. Not in the art world where tastes, at best, were fickle and had little to do, anymore, with how good you were or how bad either for that matter. Overnight he became the "Modigliani of the Mean Streets," the "Gauguin of the Gutter," at least in Chicago. A joke in itself. No one looked less like a denizen of the demimonde than Malcolm. He looked like a poster boy WASP, fair haired, blue eyed, tall and gangly, honest, thoughtful, helpful, friendly. His show, which he padded with other portraits of street people, adding a jagged scar to the face of some sad soul in a slum, changing smiles into leers, or planting a knife or a gun in a beggar's outstretched hand, had all but sold out.

That fame didn't stick. Malcolm never followed with another trick. He had already had a belly full of it and it made him sick. No trick no treat in art biz. Which nowadays was the same as showbiz: embalmed sharks or painted porcelain cartoon characters which were offered as pricey sculptures, kitsch or shock. But being a jerk had worked. He had made a name and dealers were willing to show him even though he was trying to be serious and wasn't of much monetary use.

Fashion passion, Malcolm brooded as he dabbled, a kind of trance, or death dance, because fashion dies before your eyes, and a blink in the "au courant" cosmos can knock you out of sync. And then what would everybody think?

Now he had to worry about what Rachael would think. Rachael was his conscience. She painted wild and barbaric abstract pieces that could have been found in the caves of France. She invented her own primordial symbols and slashed them across the canvas like a pre-historical guru. They were a marvel. Here he was with all that soul-felt inspiration to draw upon selling out again. Angel food cake was what he was attempting. But could anyone blame him? Nag, nag, nag, the answer to that was an easy one.

His Devil's food cake bake-off was how his romance with Rachael began, the angel and the bad man. Out into the angry night about a year after his smary, big splash, out from another mind-numbing space in the midst of his resolve to go straight, where fashion passion had once again replaced thought, feeling, grace, and money had replaced taste, Malcolm had gone reeling and screaming with a convert's outrage only to be confronted by his own disgrace.

"Monet! Renoir! Van Gogh! Gauguin!"

Malcolm had shouted his frustration to no one, everyone, anyone, at the top of his lungs. He had had too much wine to drink. La grape kept flowing at the upscale gallery opening, along with the mind-numbing art babble, two indulgences his essentially poet's head never had been able to handle. Wine made his brain fizzy, art talk made it dizzy.

"Richter! Hopper! Pollock! De Kooning!" The featured works at the avant-garde art show had been like looking at human innards through somebody's butt hole. "Rembrandt! DaVinci! Michaelangelo!" This latest concoction of the neo-insane had been especially lame – creature features, amusement park stuff without a glimmer of skill or talent, a clown act. "Rilke! Tolstoy! Kafka!" Malcolm threw in a few writers. Why not? Literature was as dead as painting or sculpture. Music too. "Beethoven! Bach! Stravinsky!"

Malcolm wanted a garden of wonderments filled with earthly delights, or Kafkaesque frights. What did the world give him? Another night of mental blight.

"Jack Daniels! Jim Beam! Johnny Walker!"

Malcolm would stop at the nearest liquor store. Those guys would help smooth things over. Nothing like a good jolt of hard liquor.

"Snoopy! Mickey Mouse! Spiderman!" Some mocking female screeched behind him. "Colonel Sanders! Long John Silver! Papa John!"

Malcolm whirled around and found some scraggly goth-girl stalking him.

"So I'm hungry." She shrugged, obviously drugged. "Mozart! Vermeer! Ibsen!"

"Beat it Vampira." Malcolm studied the dungeon-decorated princess who, for God knows what reason, was shadowing him. He had seen her before, somewhere, but why or when he couldn't remember. "Go drive your parents nuts."

He turned with a sneer and staggered away from the cryptic creature.

"Double murder! Blood sucker! Grave robber!" The banshee screeched in his ears. "Exploiter! Necrophiliac! Bottom feeder!"

Suddenly he remembered. It was that witchy looking girl from his old art school whom he had granted an interview during his show and who wrote scathing columns about his exhibit in the student newspaper.

"Nag, nag, nag." Malcolm gallows laughed. "Give it up already screaming Mimi."

"Sell out! Sell out! Sell out!" She shouted.

"Jesus! What's it to you?"

Malcolm whirled around and looked Rachael up and down, dumbfounded.

"We had a class together."

"So what?"

"I thought you were cool."

Was he done? Malcolm wondered as he squinted at the painting he was working on. Less would be more with this one – less passion, less meaning, just a suggestion, like a memory, or a dream of midnight and moonbeams. It looked good to him. The window had darkened. It was "cocktail time." Rachael would drag in soon. No job, no prospects, no follow up interviews as usual. They had both been there, done that, a thousand times; no teaching jobs, no menial jobs, no employment of any kind. Buddy can you spare a dime? Their parents had supplied the dimes, without being asked, from time to time, which made them both feel like failures and moochers. At least they weren't mooching at home but had a hovel of their own.

At cocktail time Rachael recently made the observation that they had become background characters in some seedy porno flick in which there wasn't much sex. "Cocktails for two" always concluded their days of misery and hopelessness. They sat cross-legged on the mattress, drank cheap booze, and talked about what it would take to make life livable: the what if's and what-so-evers, the maybe's and when's, until they got to the nitty gritty of all their problems.

"You're a jerk!"

"You're a screwball!"

"I should have known you were a loser!"

"Beggars can't be choosers!"

The clock ticked as they each got in their licks, taking turns pouring and chain smoking cigarettes, until the fog settled in as they ran out of gin.

"I've had it!"

"Let's end it!"

Each night the same conversation.

Each day the never-ending recession.

Each moment trapped in a hopeless situation

Malcolm signed his romantic concoction. It looked like a scene from "Lifetime for Women" perhaps with a little Hallmark Valentine's Day mixed in. It was well done. That gave him some consolation. Malcolm thought he better hide it before Rachael got home, bury it in the back of a stack Rachael would never check. Instead he dug out his cell phone and took a picture of it and beamed it to his dealer along with a text message. "Can you use this? Sofa size. If so can I get an advance? 5 Bennies maybe? Should retail at 5K." "Pretty." Came back in a flash. "I'll hit my snowbirds before they fly away. I'll bet 5 B's on this one. Check in the mail." "Make it out to Rachael." Malcolm shot back. "Tell her you sold that little piece of hers, 'Spectrum.' I'll pick it up when I bring this in."

The miracles of high tech. Malcolm hid his painting, wrote CONGRATULATIONS!! on another sofa-sized canvas amidst multicolored painted balloons and hung it in the living room. He called Wong's for a delivery of Chinese food.

"THE PAWNSHOP"

"Twins ride a see-saw, as storm clouds gather over them. Each catches a glimpse, in turn, above the other, of a star on the horizon. The grim one ponders hers and finds profound insights through it. The happy one peeks at her own, bewildered and bemused, until it finally shines on her too. It is the star of life, for one magic, for the other a wonder of science and physics. Each, identical in every way except for the way their brains were arranged, balances and enables the other in their teeter-totter journey to nowhere. As they ride up and down under the clouding night sky, the grim one sees that soon her star will vanish in the storm. Her sibling will see that, too, but only when hers is covered and is gone. The lonely cry of a train's whistle wails by like a one note lullaby."

Heather paused in her reading to push away another avalanche of chestnut hair that had tumbled across her glistening face, veiling her vision, puffing out strands with each word, as she gripped the wobbly podium, which Michael must have borrowed from some rescue gospel mission, and to swallow an ice cold mouthful of bottled water, which went down the pipe, just right, as her grandfather used say of his whiskey, which she wished she were drinking instead. In the back of the room, resplendent in diamonds, rubies, sapphires, emeralds, and every other pricey doodad she could attach to her voluptuous, platinum-haired, tanning salon, presence, her rival gazed at her haughtily, yawning periodically as she fanned herself with the night's program. Now and then, the Gold Coast socialite would turn to smile flirtatiously at Michael who stood by the door looking, as usual, like the count of some mysterious somewhere or other, dressed like a pasha in a flamboyant

186

silk woven evening jacket, camel hair slacks and cashmere turtleneck, set off by a hypnotist-sized diamond ring and solid gold watch, all unclaimed remains from the clandestine hoardings of his father's hock shop (the watch probably left by Midas) to greet any latecomers held up by the snowstorm. Heather suspected that Pasha and Prima Divorcia (she must be hitting fifty by the record of her mega buck marriage hops, although she looked no older than Heather due to the miracle of cosmetic surgery) had slept together last night, one swept away by the moment (everyone *had* been a little drunk) the other using her well-worn witch broom to fly another conquest to her magic midnight bedroom. It was apparent by the smug look (or was that the only expression that's left after your umpteenth facelift?) she had directed at Heather when she made her grand entrance and handed Connie, Michael's assistant, her sable for safe keeping.

"Years pass." Heather continued. "Each sister is now far from her home in Kansas."

The gathering of Chicago aristocrats, seated in rows of folding chairs before her in the brightly-lit, steam-hissing cellar, looked like nothing so much as a comedy skit — some parody one might find on *Saturday Night Live* or *Comedy Central*. She couldn't stop the imp that flashed a smile across her lips. "Is there something wrong with this picture?" should be the caption under the photographs the Tribune was taking for its "Society" feature. She wondered if the spread would also include the front entrance? Michael had never removed the three balls that hung above his father's pawn shop when he converted the space into an art place – "So the little shop of sorrows became a bargain basement of miracles." He said, with a shrug, when she asked about the incongruity. "It's still a place of lost souls and dreams and it's still all about money, sadly. Like the pawn guy says on TV. 'Everything here has a story and a price.' Instead of my desk I probably should transact sales behind a cage wearing my father's visor, sleeves rolled up. Besides it lends a touch of Duchamp to the ambience."

All dressed to the nines in Dior and Armani, the tycoons and Grande Dames sat uncomfortably, sweated profusely, and listened politely to (of all things) poetry recited by a banshee-haired, pixy-faced PhD. She still looked, she knew, at twenty-eight, more like the freckle-faced daughter of the Keebler elf than Big Jim McMahon's brat kid, runt of the litter that she was. "I wanted Heather to learn the construction business and someday take over," her father had told the revelers at her doctoral graduation celebration. "She's got more brains than her brothers. They'll be the first to admit it. But she kissed the blarney stone instead, disappointing her old dad. Well, the world got a great poet and a pretty one at that. What she creates with words will last longer than what I put together with brick and mortar." Not yawning, yet, but fanning themselves with their programs, as much to stay awake as combat the heat, her audience sat wondering what they had gotten themselves into as they listened to her rant. Now and then, they would turn their bewildered attention to blink at the mural-sized paintings of barrio life that surrounded them. Depicting, in clashing colors and expressionistic figures, drug lords and drive-bys, hookers, beggars, gangsters, horror, squalor, and other urban nightmares, the pieces were created by the Hispanic inner-city high school student, whom Michael had awarded, out of his own impecunious pockets (which were about as deep as a conversation with the platinum haired "Black Widow" would be if she got stuck talking with her later at the festivities) a full scholarship for art to whatever Chicago academy was his wish. There were two more such prizes, totally exhausting, she learned, his entire savings, one for poetry, in which she was the judge, the other for science.

"Diego Rivera," Michael had whispered to her that day they had strolled together through the settlement house exhibit where the young man's works were on display, "with a touch of Hieronymus Bosch thrown in?"

"And maybe a few amphetamines?" She mused, looking around at the chaos of colors and figures, which could easily get the kid arrested for assault and battery to the senses.

"And maybe a few more again." Michael laughed. "This is bravura work, an artist taking on his own inner demons while he battles social injustice in the process. I'll check out the rest of the students on my short list but I'm sure I'm done." Michael frowned. "I know art isn't supposed to make statements anymore and each of this kid's works is a Holocaust, with no let up. Not one like my father's. You couldn't even *make* art out of that! That story was best told by newspaper photographers, documentary film makers or young girls who kept diaries while hiding in attics from Nazis. This is riveting stuff, packed with the pathos, and all the tragedy being human can be. I could see these gut level recreations of ghetto life coming but I didn't suspect so many would be so good. I knew, of course, I would be taken by whatever came in. But, then, Jews don't have to bend their brains much to find beauty in such visual nightmares. They were born to a surrealist dream and they bear the legacy of their exotic genes, which lend themselves to Symbolist renderings. Besides, a bit mashuguna is what everyone I ever knew thought of me." ('Gee, I wonder why Michael?' She refrained from commenting. 'Can it be because you do things like give away all your money?') 'That's what many of the *real* art experts think I am anyway. Art for me has to involve itself in humanity, express feelings, emotions, not word games or mind games. They don't agree. But what do I know? I'm just a small time art dealer, the son of a Holocaust survivor turned pawnbroker. I guess empathy is my eccentricity. Much of what they show looks like funhouse stuff to me and maybe belongs more to an amusement park than a museum or art gallery. Contemplation doesn't follow the confrontation no matter how jolting that may be. Maybe they're mashuguna? In any event, now that the mayor and the leading citizens have generously agreed to take over the scholarship competition, I guess because it drew some local and national attention, and make it an annual event, actually adding a few more categories to the grants, they can pick their own judges and do what they want. Traditional cityscapes, avant-garde experiments, whatever turns them on. It will be their call from now on. I just wanted to get this project off the ground. I'm not even sure why. After ten years of dealing art, a situation that came about by accident, I found that I had half a million dollars in the bank and, since my needs are small, nothing I could think of to spend it on. I suppose I could have expanded my business. Instead, I did this. I'm not sure I know what art is anyway. Who does these days? A curator at the museum told me they call *au courant* endeavors 'spaghetti.' They throw it all at the wall and see what sticks. All I know is that what I like affects me deeply. But maybe it's just a pawn in a game? And a big money one. In which case the three balls above my door are appropriate. I may know writing. I'm the classic caricatured Jewish bookworm. That art form only works if it says something. Your book, 'Leprechauns in the Attic,' is a joy. That's why I came to you. Your words, the people that inhabit the poetry of your Gaelic-magical-realism world, with all its myths and folk lore, paradox, irony, joy, tragedy, mystery … the migration of the Irish Catholics from the potato famine to the present … the lace curtain years to the nouveau riche … the ironies and satires of the American dream … are roses in a garden one doesn't weed, because the wild growth is as much of a wonderment as the tended part is. This kid's urban jungle has such flowers in it and those moments of magical truth."

"Gee thanks, Michael." Heather remembered thinking as she looked around at the blazing walls which threatened to explode. "An unweeded garden." Maybe she should use that quote for the back of her next book? Maybe she should use it for the title? *My Unweeded Garden* by *Heather McMahon.* But there *was* a wild beauty in the Hispanic youth's works. They were violent but poignant, filled with heart stabbing portraits of impoverished families in the backgrounds, trying to live their dreams, and sad-eyed children lost in a bedlam. The poems were the same, touching and disturbing. If the aristocrats thought they were being tortured now, Heather mused as she watched them glance around furtively, wait until *her* winner, a seventeen-year-old African American girl seated in the first row with her invalid mother next to the mayor, dressed almost as a counterpoint to her gritty text in austere Sunday-go-to-meeting attire, a frail, timid creature, read *her* works.

"All bitter pills to swallow I'll bet." Michael had sympathized with her as she waded through the "short list" the panel had sent her – which wasn't exactly short: fifty poets with five works each. It wasn't that the works were difficult. They weren't loaded with metaphors, symbolism or references that one had to ponder or decipher. They hit you like a sock in the jaw. They made you shiver and, if not cry, sometimes brought a tear to your eye.

> I walk among the lost,
> where chasms have no bridges,
> over bottomless abysses.
> I live alongside the longing.
> I live amidst the yearning,
> side by side with the struggling,
> in the ghettos and the grottos
> of misery and suffering.
> I am that haunt you sense in the
> mirror. I am you in despair.

or:

> Hustle or muscle – that's the
> only way for the boys to get
> by in the ghetto: deal, steal,
> pimp, kill – each day the same

191

ole crime of being alive.
Bars without spaces to look
through surround you. That's
because no one outside wants
to see your misery, hear your
cries ... that deaf ear, blind eye,
as you slowly die.

Not exactly "Ode to a Grecian Urn," but effective, nevertheless. They were sleeping together by then. It hadn't taken long. Life comes at you quick. Ironic, since she had wanted no part of this obscure "art dealer's" scholarship competition to begin with. Although the honorarium was generous. It seemed like a gimmick, some promotional stunt some "Shylock" on the make cooked up. She turned Michael's letter of request down with the warmest wishes for the competition's success, begging off due to prior commitments. Her excuse was valid. She was already swamped with similar requests, as well as those for readings, lectures, panel discussions, from colleges and universities throughout the country. Since the university had published her book, which had received much praise and numerous awards, she was in big demand. Maybe big amends was a better angle, her slender volume receiving a kind of compensatory recognition for past women writers the field had neglected? Whatever, the dean, whom had gotten wind of the request for Michael's contest, ultimately talked her into it. There was a lot of "buzz around town" about the competition, he informed her. The president's speech on his "agenda for academic excellence" had inspired the art dealer according to the papers. Obama had mentioned and thanked the generous small business benefactor from his home town Chi-town, the city of big shoulders and hearts and urged others, if they could, to follow this good citizen's example. Involving herself in something that was garnering a fair amount of attention would be good for her book, the dean pointed out, as well as the university. The winners were going to appear on various television programs. "Maybe the judges too?" He mused. Hinting at a prospect no writer could refuse.

"One twin lives in New York and is a scientist."

Michael was gone. Connie stood in his place by the door next to the security guard. He said he would slip out for a drink when the proceedings got going, brace himself for the ensuing commotion. "You know how I hate schmoozing." He winced. "A couple of stiff ones in some quiet place will get me through it."

"The other resides in LA and is an artist."

Heather couldn't possibly guess what would show up at her office, when she finally caved into the dean. She still thought there was something fishy about the whole thing. No one shelled money out of their own pocket unless they expected a payback. She felt like she was being played – these students, too. To start something that would get the attention of the president and local, as well as, national newscasts was pretty shrewd. Maybe some bon vivant wearing an ascot and a beret? Some flim-flam man with a con artist grin? Some Hollywood wannabe wearing shades, a toupee, and calling her and everyone else "babe?" What walked in was a magician, tall, dark, handsome. But, despite the high-style clothes and mesmerist's ring, he didn't seem like a guy who had something up his sleeve. Later, after she got to know him better (and Michael explained that he wore his glad rags and assorted accoutrements because he accidently discovered – Michael seemed to discover everything accidently – trying on garments and sundry ornaments from the pawnshop's storage bin for fun, that the outlandish concoctions impressed his clients and helped sell paintings) that first impression of a mystical esthetic, slowly became somewhat altered. The dark devouring eyes, starving for truth, beauty, the meaning of life, not acquisitions, the biblical aquiline nose, sensuous lips, formed a semblance belonging more to someone lost and searching than a practitioner of the black arts and hocus pocus. At forty, Michael's face retained some kind of the wayward poster child persona of a wandering soul looking in a window, maybe, shadowy, haunting, searching for a doorway to get out of the cold. Which was understandable given his neglected childhood, which sounded like a tale Charles Dickens might have written. It would have made her want to adopt him even if she hadn't already taken him for her lover. It was the main reason she hadn't strangled him yet or turned him over to her construction worker brothers, who would have given him a friendly warning of what would come if he ever gave their sister the runaround. Beware Black Widow, she mused, the fighting Irish was in her, too.

"Where on earth did you get this bed, Michael, a fire sale at the Cook County jail? You know with half a million dollars you could have gotten a pretty good mattress. At least one without lumps. I guess you never thought of that?"

"Not really. I suppose I'm used to it."

"And your lovers?"

"They don't seem to notice. Too preoccupied with other things. If you know what I mean?"

"Sure, get right on to the pleasure principle and avoid the pain. Well we better get at it. I'm on top."

He proved to be a magician in bed, both his lumpy one and hers, as well as numerous others over the years, she came to learn. He seemed to run into old flames everywhere they went, bars, nightclubs, restaurants, amidst the glitter of their Gold Coast jaunts. "Michael! How good to see you! Robbing the cradle as usual? And you must be one of his new artists. Fresh out of school are you? You'll enjoy Michael. He's a maestro. Don't enjoy him too much, it will be over before you know it."

So, he was hocus pocus after all. Now you see him, now you don't, according to the gossip that went around. A master of the vanishing act. Houdini with a hard-on? No. His psychological problems, she came to observe, went deeper than that. He was an escape artist – from responsibility, commitment, from any domestic involvement, from

194

realities of every kind, especially if they involved the ties that bind. Intimacy was not his forte. Empathy maybe, but not if it involved him other than existentially. He was afraid of it. She suspected that that was why he had suddenly gotten the urge to give away his money. It was a grand gesture, of course. He *was* kind-hearted, nice in every way. But the money was a trap. At forty he had to do something life changing with it – settle down, get married, raise a family. Become a real businessman. He had gotten into art as a lark. "I had this dead end, monotonous job as a supervisor in a medical records department, something my half-brother – you met him, the surgeon – got for me. It was OK. At that age, I was an aspiring writer anyway. I still think I have one book in me. Then my father, unexpectedly, left me his little property when he died which, since the neighborhood went so upscale, is worth a lot of money. A million dollars probably. All I had to do was maintain it and pay taxes. This being Chicago's main art district, I went with the flow and to my amazement became fairly successful."

What was amazing to Heather wasn't his success as an art dealer but his total lack of introspection as a voracious reader and aspiring writer. He needed a shrink for a girlfriend not a PhD of poetry. Anyone could see that the art he was attracted to was exactly what he lacked in his personality – feeling, or a running commitment to it. He was caring, affectionate, loving, with someone, for a small intense time, it seemed, then he drifted away, back to his lost soul state. A shadow on the loose with no one to claim it. Yet he was drawn by these compassionate renderings like a moth to a flame. He was a connoisseur of such haunting sentiments captured with paint. The artists he represented were magnificent. Their works were wonderments. They were moving, often disturbing. Each one captured profound truths in some way whether by fable, or the surreal, or the expressionistic, or representational, about being human. She loved hanging out there surrounded by them. The two of them together as if in some wondrous dream, which was why they usually ended up staying together there rather than her plush new condo with its view of the lake. Even the lumpy bed and his small, cozy living space in the back seemed an extension of the gallery's nether world ambience. The walls were packed floor to ceiling with old, gilt-framed black and white photographs of the building, the pawnshop, life along the surrounding streets taken, judging by the clothes and cars, mostly in the late forties and fifties, and filled, she assumed, with family, friends, relations, many Orthodox Jews, the men bearded, the women wearing extravagant hats. Rag- or junk-filled wagons rolled through many of the antique street scenes drawn by horses wearing funny hats.

"Back in the day," Michael mused as they lay together and gazed at the photographs, "my mother owned the whole building. That is with her first husband. That's their wedding portrait above the menorah. My mother, as you can see, was very beautiful. What you can't see is that she was lame. She dragged her right foot after her until the end of her days. Their marriage was arranged. Marriage brokers weren't uncommon in those days. The groom was the same age as her father. He has a kind face and it was a good match, since he was a landlord and the owner of a pawnshop. It was the best one she could get with her foot. They lived right here behind the shop. They both worked it. The rest of the brownstone comprised a small, seedy, backstreet hotel where street hookers would rent rooms by the hour to service their customers and down and out transients flopped for a couple of bucks. The whole neighborhood was seedy back then, as you can tell from the pictures – the streets filled with gin mills, strip joints, greasy spoons, pawnshops. Now it's gentrified. You can find some of that old Chicago ambience near the YMCA along Chicago Avenue or by its intersection with Clark. At night, it's still something of a no man's land, at least for a couple of blocks. My father entered the picture later. He's that brute over there with the bushy eyebrows and thick curly hair. He was the son of a butcher in a village in Czechoslovakia. Most of the village, all of his family, were exterminated in the camps. He survived because at fourteen he was as big as a man, with a thick neck and huge hands and of course the stamina of youth which enabled him to get through a year and a half of that hell on earth. They put him to work on a labor crew and used his muscles for the Fuhrer. By the time the camps were liberated, he was dead inside. Their marriage was arranged by a broker, as well. My mother was a new widow then with two children, my half brother and sister. She needed a man, and a big one at that, who could take care of business and with his fists if it came to that. The neighborhood was still bad. In some ways, it was worse, or at least wilder. Glittering strips of gangster-owned nightclubs were springing up everywhere, bringing swarms of revelers, along with pickpockets, muggers, drug dealers. Baby boomer teenagers, many from rough neighborhoods, roamed the streets in gangs. My father, a Mallet Man at the stockyards, that's the guy who killed the cattle with a spiked sledge hammer as they were herded down the fenced off aisles, was out of work. The yards were rapidly closing down. Initially, he was brought to America by distant relatives. They tried to set him up as a kosher butcher. But that didn't last long. He was a drunkard and a brawler. The camps, first Auschwitz, then Buchenwald, had turned an amiable but somewhat slow-witted boy into a monster. If looks could kill? You can see murder in his eyes in his wedding photograph and all the rest. It's the only look he ever gave me, or my mother or anyone. It was frightful being around him, especially when he was drunk, which was often. Who can blame him after living surrounded by barbed wire and witnessing beatings, hangings, mass shootings and the human smoke billowing from the crematoriums. I hold nothing against him. They made the contract. He learned the business, collected the rents, scared off thugs and robbers probably simply with his presence. He helped raise, in his own way, the two kids. I came along next, unexpected and uninvited. They were middle-aged by then. Bernie, the oldest, was Bar

Mitzvah that year. Rhonda, as beautiful as my mother, was popular, a big hit at school with oodles of young boys chasing after her even then. She married well. They both did well. No scars inflicted that I can tell. My parents seemed to have had little to do with each other. He had his whores, loose women, kept to himself. They lived together like work mates, survivors of a hard fate.

Maybe drunk one night he forced her? Who can say? I never felt like a son to either of them. I was something unwanted. Maybe the product of a regretful rape?

My mother died of cancer when I was ten. My father converted all the flats into condominiums, including the one we all lived in and sold them to put Bernie and Rhonda through college. Bernie's education, of course, went on and on and cost a small fortune. My father and I moved down here. I learned the business, worked my way through a useless BA at Circle campus, took the job my brother got for me. Sometime I'll show you the root cellar. It's a little storage space dug out under the basement. You get there through a trap door in the floor, covered over by that Persian rug. That was my room. The walls are cork-lined That's where I get all my glad rags from."

As well as his "sad rags" – Heather lamented, that inability to keep a deep relationship. He told her later that he was often locked down there by his father. Sometimes as a punishment or when his father wanted to party with his women or friends. He would come in late at night, glare at him and point at the trap door and then shove a heavy chest over it to make sure Michael wouldn't go to the washroom and bother them. He peed in a can. Whatever else was his life she could only imagine. It was a lonely life, lived mostly through books, roaming the streets when he could. When he was older, he told her, he went to the museum a lot. What he liked about that experience, almost as much as the art, was being around the patrons, bright-looking and well-dressed. A relieving contrast to the sad souls who came into the pawnshop to hock their poor treasures. Heather flashed on the poem that made her pick her winner.

> Dead of winter, shadowing down
> streets as black as any nightmare,
> although it wasn't even time for supper.
> "I got dizzy, Sweetie."
> "I knows Mama."
> She came home from school and found
> her mother on the floor. Her baby
> brother and sister stood there by her,
> scared. They had gotten home first,
> tried to lift her. Impossible when the
> dead weight of the curse was on her.
> They couldn't find her pills. They
> brought her blankets and pillows.
> "Where's your purse Mama?"
> "I ain't got no money, Honey."
> Her mother looked ashen, like the
> embers of coal burned.
> "I needs to get your medicine."
> "I ain't got no more. I was going
> to the drugstore."
> Her purse was on the floor, right
> next to her, covered by the blanket.
> There were no more pills in the vile
> she kept tucked away at its bottom.
> "I get you a refill." She pocketed the
> container. "You two sup on that lunch
> meat wrapped up in the fridge." She told
> her siblings. "Get Mama some tea. I

bring you back some candy."
By now every predator was out there,
prowling through the icy dark: rapists,
muggers, gangbangers, killers. She
pulled on her winter coat, cap, mittens.

The contest was an ordeal. Michael's stories were an ordeal. They made her reflect on her own youthful years. One summer in her teenhood made her shudder. How arrogant they were, all of them, she and her friends, so full of themselves in their privileged lives and pretenses. Her parents were affluent. She grew up in a big house on the North Shore. Nothing was denied her, or her siblings or any of their friends. There was travel, country clubs in which to swim and play the summers away, private schools, mentors, tutors, Barnard eventually, shopping sprees with her friends in the plush suburban malls or along Chicago's beyond upscale "Magnificent Mile," concerts, museums. When she was sixteen she and a few of her schoolmates formed a fun trio and billed themselves "The Ghetto Girls." They dressed funky, sang rap songs, which she cooked up lampooning the North Shore, the Gold Coast and making parallels to their "sisters" in the slums. They sang at weddings, parties, dances, the country club once, anywhere they could stand in front of a band. They were so cute, clever. They were a big hit that summer. They didn't mean anything bad by it. What were they thinking? How embarrassing to have as a memory now. What was that Categorical Imperative by Kant? "…whatever we do or say or think should be a moral imperative for all humanity … our slightest whim or action … a transcendental law for all time …"

"Still identical in body and soul," Heather gave her winner a smile, signaling that she was finishing so take a deep breath because you are up next, "although what each does is often mistaken for an opposite pursuit," she wanted to tie in the art and science aspect of the scholarships, "the twins still balance and in turn lift one another to get a glimpse of that star."

Of course it behooved her to thank everyone, after the applause finished, for attending the first of an ongoing commitment to Chicago's inner city high school students – their graciousness and generosity, while at the same time reflecting that they wouldn't have to drag themselves out in the snow, sit sweating in an overheated cellar and shell out dough, if they simply paid their employees, in all those enterprises and factories they owned, a better wage so they could take care of themselves; or maybe just pay their fair share of the taxes so the government could handle it.

All around Michael in the night, like icicles dangling from the winter sky, towers rose, sleek with glass and reflections of the nebulous. Strolling below, amidst the parks, gardens, walks, fountains, the quaint Victorian mansions and smug old brownstones – most of which had been converted into pricey eateries, watering holes and Gold Coast condos – began to assume an illusion of fairyland as a heavenly lake effect snow descended on Chicago and flakes as big as dove feathers transformed the spires and gables into enchanted castles.

Michael glanced at his Midas watch and slipped into the posh, park nightclub. Within, tourists, travelers, amiable neighborhood residents were sipping cocktails and watching the magic show from the ornate French windows as they listened to the piano echo the dream outside with its mellow notes.

"Now you know what it means to be alone."

The North Shore Chanteuse was wailing her tales of sorrow like some god forsaken angel as he found a small table in a corner, ordered a drink, and waited for the jeweler, who would meet him soon.

"A broken heart
A dream that fell apart"

201

The track lights above the golden-voiced beauty glimmered like moon glow. Seated atop a black piano, her intonations, breathless, tragic, her sultry figure smothered under cascades of silvery hair that fell like rain showers across her shoulders, as she whispered her dark melodies of love and rapture, while women wept and men sat mesmerized and Michael wondered again, as he wondered when he was dating her, how such a cold, stone-hearted, bitch could capture and deliver such soul shattering loveliness? Go figure artists!

A homeless family, bundled in rags and carrying bags, shuffled through the park searching for somewhere to settle for the night, a small stone bridge over a stream, maybe, which they could use as a shelter, or if they really got lucky, a park maintenance shack for which they could easily jimmy the lock. They trudged through the drifts into the darkness and disappeared into the falling snow and frozen unknown.

Meshuguna. Michael brooded. Reality was crazy, always had been, always would be. "The poor are always with us." Some luminary noted. So are the oppressed. So are luminaries come to think of it. He was broke, wiped out, kaput. He lifted his drink in a silent salute to his father, to all the persecuted Jews over all the ages and to all others who had been enslaved, cleansed, exterminated, tortured, abused, wherever they were, had been, would be, forever and amen. It was for them he had given up his money, all the oppressed of humanity. At least that was his notion. He had looked into a madman's eyes since childhood – his father's eyes, pondered that grim expression, those numbers scrawled on his arm. He felt ashamed of himself. Why? He couldn't say. The survivor syndrome? Because he became wealthy easily? What did the world look like to the lumbering village boy after the hell he lived in those camps? He always wondered. Each face a phantom version of a human face? Each figure ghostly? Every street a shaft of smoke and mirrors? Every moment inimical? He had to make that grand gesture. He had to make it also for the poor souls who came to the pawnshop everyday to pawn what they held dearly. Thank god no one was after the Jews anymore, he reflected, except investment bankers and luxury car dealers. They were safe here and most everywhere. Those persecution days were finally over. They were safe in Israel, too, on the whole. Despite their relentless enemies on all sides. They took care of each other. On his fortieth birthday, he decided to give away his money, sell the gallery and move there. For forty years, he had lived like a ghost in a dream, not a real person, certainly not his own. He wasn't even sure what that could be. He had no friends as a kid. He had to hurry home and help his father, who became more wasted every year, take care of the shop. He had no family to speak of – his half brother and sister were all but out of the house when he was born and soon they were gone. College, marriage, their busy lives went on separate from his own. When they did get together, on holidays or other occasions, he never felt comfortable. He didn't fit in. Religion had ended when his mother died. His father hated God. He wouldn't set foot in a synagogue. Who could blame him? How else would one feel about the grand master of it all after what he'd been through, what he'd seen? Michael was an atheist. The mysteries of existence belonged to and were solved by science. The revelations they came up with were far more amazing than the visions of old time mystics. We are all orphans, lost or abandoned in a land at once dangerous and enchanted. All we have is one another to rely on. We are our own angels and demons. Prayer is a shelter made of wind, salvation earth bound, sermons words and images that are heart-found, not handed down. Not that he wasn't moved by cantors' voices, the ceremonies and services, the poetry in the prayers, the candles, rituals, the rabbis' thoughtful proverbs. He was, of course, moved by all passionate expressions of the inner world and its longings. What he yearned for was that Sabbath sense of sacredness and spirituality, everyday in a secular way and that feeling of mutual identity in a community. He was a genetic Jew. No one would take him for anything else. It was written all over his face, embedded in his being. He thought if he moved to Israel he might find a home, inner peace. America was a giddy Disneyland with showbiz on the one end and make-believe on the other, glued together by greed – most of his brethren no exception. He needed something real after his life in a shadow world, some shared community that was meaningful. Even the art world, which he had enjoyed being part of for many years, was going sour on him. The current big guns were shrouded in the mystique of investment manipulations. There *was* no literary world. No one read outside the academies. Everyone was glued to the boob tube or arcade-style computer games. There was little left, especially in politics, that wasn't bogus. When he was young, America was number one in everything – science, culture, education. Now they were at, or heading toward, the bottom. The students ranked lower than any westernized country on test scores, while they were firing teachers and cutting down on grants and programs! The outlook for the future was pretty gloomy. He wasn't lonely. Maybe existentially. It had been a long time ago that he roamed the streets of Chicago with his hands in his pockets, head down, wishing he had a friend. There had been too many women to fill his time since then. But with them there was always something missing. Maybe something in him? If so, that was at an end.

"Sorry I'm late." Zubrowsky, the jeweler, suddenly appeared at the table looking like a Jewish polar bear. He was covered, head to foot, with snow. His glasses were fogged. His red nose dripped. He stomped his boots on the carpet, slapped his fur hat against his leg. "I couldn't get a cab. Buses passed me like sardine cans with engines. I had to walk the whole way. They announced on the radio a blizzard for Chicago. People are fleeing the city. I don't know how I'll get home if it doesn't calm down. I almost couldn't find this place. I walked in circles. The world got erased."

"Good god Zub." Michael stood and helped him out of his coat. It was really coming down now, just in the last few minutes. He hadn't noticed. In the windows was a white out. Swirling flakes filled the air.

204

"Have a drink, warm up. You should have called me. We could have put it off."

"Put it off? Rush you said! A rush job! Life and death!"

"Well, maybe it wasn't that dramatic." Michael smiled. "Just seemed like tonight would be the perfect time. But have a seat. Relax. Let's see it!"

Zubrowsky sat and took a velvet box out of his suit jacket, Groucho Marxed his bushy eyebrows and laid it on the table.

"Well open it. Don't just stare at it. It's a big step, I know, but they won't bite you."

The diamond rings were dazzling. They made Michael's hands tremble as he studied them under the light of the table candle. Legend had it that the stones belonged to a giant ring, owned by a very prominent woman who had to give them up during the Great Depression, which Michael had Zubrowky reset into an engagement ring and wedding band. He had been astonished to have found them still in his father's hoardings. Maybe he was saving them for his old age? Maybe with his heavy drinking, black outs, and foggy thinking, he had simply forgotten about them. They were worth a small fortune.

"God they're beautiful!" Michael marveled.

"So tonight it is you pop the question?" Zubrowsky sipped his drink, pleased at the reaction to his handiwork. "There's two ways to do it. There's the Gentile way and the Jewish way. The Gentile gets down on one knee, takes the woman's hand and asks her for it. If she accepts he slips on her finger the ring with a kiss. If she says no he bows politely and goes. The Jewish way is exactly the same only the ring is shown before he asks anything. More impact, get it? Hedging your bet. I'm just kidding, Michael! I'm making a joke! But in your case maybe you should think about it. It would put a little oomph into the proposition. Why take chances? Ice like that you might convince her. I'm just kidding again! Well Mazel Tov." He drained his drink. "I'm off. Keep in touch. I'll mail you the bill. No charge for the delivery. A little extra maybe for the doctor when he treats me for frostbite and pneumonia. Send me an invite! Good night!.""

It *was* a big step. Michael's heart pounded as he turned the sparkling box this way and that, watching its multicolored diamonds catch fire under the flickering flame in all their facets. He kept picturing Heather wearing them and how they would sparkle on her hand in classrooms, at lectures, out to dinner, the theater, whatever. Of course, she was always smiling in his imagination but actually Michael was afraid she wouldn't even like them. They were sort of over the top – more than a bit ostentatious. She didn't wear much jewelry, make-up or showy clothes either. Her tastes were simpler, what you would call prim and proper. She got that from her mother and grandmother and beyond that, probably from ancestral Irish how to act-like-a-lady instructions. Prim and proper, that was Heather, except, of course, for her hair which, no matter what she did with it, made her look like she had just stuck her finger into an electric socket.

"Shocking, say it, shocking!" she'd scream getting dressed for a night out and glaring at her reflection in the mirror while she dragged a brush through its tangles, the bristles of which Michael wasn't sure he'd use on a horse's mane.

"Your hair is becoming."

"Becoming? Oh really? For what, a clown's fright wig, or the lead singer in an Irish rebel band? My hair is exploding!"

"Your hair is very sexy."

"Then why don't you ever run your fingers through it?"

"Don't I?"

He supposed he could try. He was afraid they might get stuck and it would be awkward trying to pull them out.

"I'm sure I do all the time. You don't notice. How could I resist?"

"That's it!" Heather slammed her brush on the dresser. "I've had it! I'm shaving my head and buying a wig! Don't your Orthodox kinswomen all wear them to cover their heads? Bet that would turn you on! You'd be a Chagall figure flying upside down!"

"You turn me on. Your hair turns me on. Everything about you sends me swooning. Look I'll run my fingers through it."

"Back off! Don't touch it! I've just spent the last hour trying to comb it!"

He'd bet her family would like the rings. They would be impressed. They weren't very impressed by him – a middle-aged Jewish art dealer who lived in a cellar. He was probably even more unsuitable as a suitor than the other unsuitable suitors: tweedy English professors, dialectic materialists, organic language deconstructionists, Heather had brought home over the years.

"Look Michael," Heather had briefed him before she sprang him on them, "my father and brothers are basically beer swilling, sports minded, dwarf tossers. Never mind the country clubs they belong to and the flashy cars they drive. Do you play golf? It doesn't matter. We'll talk about the scholarship you're sponsoring. After all, that's how we got together. My mother will find it romantic, and noble. My father is an ardent Democrat. You know he and Richie are buddies, as was my grandfather and Richard the elder. They've worked on big contracts for the city, and will do more. They're friends now with Emanuel. We'll steer the conversation toward politics – the Tea Party, Birthers, Republicans in general, Sarah, Fox news. He won't even notice you're not Irish. There's nothing to be anxious about. Just don't tell them you gave away your last penny. Or any money."

So, courting was ever easy? Her parents were nice. Her father was a stand-up guy. So were her brothers. There would be no problem there. They all knew he loved Heather and that she loved him. They were made for each other. She had moxie. He had chutzpah, sort of. They were both mashuguna. "Why don't you call your next book 'Leprechauns In The Bed?' Michael kidded. "Meaning?" "Meaning Ms. Prim and Proper acts pixilated when she gets under the covers. "Complaining?" "Hardly – exclaiming!" They read together, discussed books, liked the same movies, music, enjoyed the company of each other like some old married couple instead of one that had just gotten together. It had been like that from the first instant, as if their relationship was a reincarnation, each moment a reenactment of sometime ancient, their togetherness something intense. "Michael, we scare me." Heather would shudder after some heated love making. "I know what you mean." Heart pounding, Michael stared at the spinning ceiling. "True love's a many scary thing."

Israel was over. He could have a life here with Heather. He couldn't imagine any other. That crazy gesture of giving away his money had brought him everything he had missed in his life and longed for. It was all like some biblical proverb. Just last night he had gotten an offer from Muriel Strand to be the new director for Strand Foundation's charitable division. "Our current head is a crook," she told him, "skimming money and cooking the books. I need someone honest." The salary for that position, he imagined, must be staggering and made his head spin. She wanted to celebrate the occasion with a night of fun and games. Bouncing around in bed with the platinum-haired socialite bombshell was quite a temptation but Michael had resisted. He confided to her that he was proposing to Heather. She laughed and said: "Michael being honest to the core can be a bore. We only demand fidelity from our directors in money matters. But that's a good sign. I'll really know my money is in good hands when you sign all those dotted lines. A woman scorned is hell to deal with but you took that risk. I'm doubly impressed."

He snapped the box shut and looked at his watch. He had better get back. Zub was right. Chicago was getting hit by a blizzard. He'd never get a cab. It was a good eight blocks to the gallery. By the time he got there he'd look like a snowman or a dybbuk come back from the dead.

"Snow White in a glass casket was what I had been aiming at with my Surrealistic portrait of the Dead Zone's crack racket, trying to symbolize the lost soul in the black hole of the ghetto, and the living-death-quest of hopelessness all around us. But the chaos of contours I created in the fairytale beauty's features, after I started slashing paint on the canvas, and the undulating rhythms of brush strokes with which I concocted her coffin, had her come out of my backstreet fable as an angel wearing a death mask of sable, asleep on a billiard table. So maybe 'Dust' was the thrust of my journey into oblivion in a game you can't win, because a drug is a drug and there's plenty of 'Dust' in the hood. Besides, while Picasso said that what one paints is what counts and not what one intended to accomplish, he also said that if you know exactly what you're going to do there's no point in going through it. Life lives as it does, I guess, and you go with the flow. I'm no Picasso, let's face it; but neither is anyone else working now. Kiefer, Richter, Viola, the late, great Munoz are my heroes, but still no Picassos. From the past, Goya is the best."

Heather wondered, anxiously, where Michael could be, as she stood amidst a handful of benefactors who had remained, despite the storm, to listen to José expound upon his paintings. He had sold three. Michael should have been there. Connie, of course, handled the sales expertly but she was getting nervous too. You could tell she was being overwhelmed. The guests had begun to slip out during her winner's recital and were all but gone by the time the pale Russian came to his science demonstration. The cellar's tiny windows looked like Whirlpool washing machines, the snow swirling, blowing, drifting in them.

"It was the dead of winter, like now, when I did this one." José rambled on, the sales, like steroids, pumping through his veins. "I looked out at the falling snow from my ghetto studio at the ragged figures roaming the streets below, dragging themselves through the drifts – bag ladies, homeless families, dead-enders. There were more each day as the recession swept the country. Rolex watches, wedding rings, good luck charms were filling the pawnshop windows as the ghetto became a 'Rainbow Coalition' like Jessie Jackson always shoots for but not in that way. So, I thought: 'Hey, fairy tales can come true and it can happen to you.' And I put down a little sketch of Hansel and Gretel and then I went loco."

Heather looked at her watch. Maybe Michael left a trail of breadcrumbs? She couldn't get him on his cell phone. Lucky for him, if she did she'd blow out his eardrum. *"I loved your reading!"* The face-lifted, bust-expanded, liposuctioned, dyed-haired, salon-tanned Grande Dame squealed at her as she was leaving. *"It was so compelling! Is that from your new book "Bats In My Belfry?"* "No. And the book is entitled 'Leprechauns In The Attic.'" *"How charming! I'll have my maid pick it up! Tell Michael I'll see him Monday. Tell him not to be tardy! I guess we can't tell a book by its cover can we?"* She studied Heather with a bemused scrutiny before she said goodnight to Connie.

What the hell did *that* mean?

The radiators were rattling, the steam hissing. The lights started blinking. But it wasn't a power out, it was Connie trying to get everyone's attention. The security guard stood next to her, arms folded, smiling.

"Ladies and Gentlemen, the weather service just announced that we are in for the biggest blizzard since nineteen sixty-seven. Remember that one? We thank you for attending, but I think we all have just a small window of opportunity, at this point, to get safely to our destinations. We bid you goodnight and safe passage. Leon will help you to your cars. Your drivers are here. Careful with the steps, they're treacherous!"

Where the hell was Michael? Heather looked at her watch again as the tycoons finished their drinks and exchanged goodbye handshakes and the snow swirled through the open door where the smiling guard stood waiting to escort the guests to their cars.

* * *

"How much?"

"Where did you get these?"

"How much?"

"I gotta know. I got to know how to go."

"I found them on a body in the alley. It's out there in the snow. How much?"

"I don't know."

The watch was solid gold. The diamond eye-blinder was worth a small fortune. They had to change, be rearranged. The watch melted down maybe. They would lose their value. That was a shame.

"A lot. I'll let you know. you got lucky. Cash too?"

"Some. Enough for a little fun."

"Have fun. A week, maybe two. The payoff will be good for both me and you."

* * *

Heather woke up when she heard the door slam. She had fallen asleep on the coach with a drink in her hand. The last of many. "Michael?" Michael stood in the gallery, shivering. He looked like a snowman.

"I never thought I'd make it home." He slapped his hat on his coat and tried to brush off the snow. "You should see it outside. My cell phone died. First it was a wonderland. Then it was no-mans-land. I thought I'd break my neck getting the cat. How'd things go?"

"Are you drunk? Do you know what I've been through? I spent the last hour calling hospital emergency rooms! Where in the hell were you?"

"In an alley mostly. I heard this cat yowling. You couldn't see your own hand if you held it in front of your face. The snow is falling that hard. But the cat was someplace high up. I climbed on top of this dumpster. I could hear it somewhere above the rain gutter. There's this old, boarded up building down the block. I think that's where I was. I couldn't reach over it so I found this window covered with grating and managed to pull myself on the ledge. I still wasn't high enough. There was a fire escape ladder another window over so I edged my way on to that. I was soaked with sweat. I climbed the rungs but they led to a dead end. There was a chimney I had to get around. I knew the cat was on the other side of that, hunkered down out of the wind."

"Michael where's the cat?"

"In my pocket." He reached down into his topcoat and pulled out a yellow and white striped kitten. "It was one, two, three after that, more or less." He handed it over to Heather. "I edged along the gutter holding onto the chimney, precariously. I snatched it up and put it in my coat but we couldn't get back to the ladder. The wind was blowing too hard. I couldn't even see the ladder. Eventually I found the dumpster and swung down onto that."

"We better feed it." The cat purred in her arms as she scratched it. "There's a bottle of milk left over from the event."

"OK. Let me get out of these things. Will you marry me?"

"OK. But look Michael I had this dream. You're not wearing that goofy watch anymore or that crazy hypnotist's ring."

"OK. I have something else for you. It's in my pocket. I hope the cat didn't do anything on top of it."

Hello.
In a word
Friendship.

THE SEARCHERS

Shadow to shadow
Each solitary soul
Listening for the beat
On the dark of another heart…

GIFT WRAPPED

Things tied with strings, or wrapped
with ribbons, my life, until the package
unraveled.
I married a dark-eyed girl, raised some
children. I lavished them in all the
nine-to-five amenities my blood, sweat
and tears could bring them – we were broke
a lot to sum it up, never broken.
Love, marriage, the baby carriage, OK
by me, both of us – our blue heaven shopping
at the seven-eleven. Anything beyond that
either flat left us or left us flat. We were
OK with that.
The great mysteries, God, existence, destiny,
were moonbeams lighting our home and
we left them alone content with the glow
they added to life in their own opaque way.
Now the man who lives here isn't there,
not in his head or bed, upon the stair or
anywhere. The dark-eyed girl is gone, maybe
to heaven, away from our blue one. Life
lingers on, she lingers on, some, in the
presence of the children whenever
I see them, which isn't very often.

HEAVENLY SHADES OF NIGHT

The Big Dream Score,
The Top Bop Jackpot,
dead as road kill,
as a rigged roulette wheel ...
No guardian angels in these dark grottos,
crypts, caverns, night world catacombs,
no mojo, ace in the hole, as the winter
winds wail like junkshop violins and winos
rummage through the streets and sanitation
trash bins, while gunfire crackles across the
Dead Zone's labyrinths.
"So, life beat you down lad?"
Says the alley cat to the sewer rat.
"What's in that? Have another drink
pal, you'll get back."
Time in a bottle – night town's broken
clock measuring planetary motion
by the shadows that prowl.
"Round, like a circle in a spiral,"
Another blind alley bar stool, another dead
end dive, where midnight angels watch
from the shadows through ocelot eyes.
"All you need is love"
Day labor dollars watching back from my
wallet like a craps shoot of snake eyes.

Candlelight flickers in the open doorway
at the top of the stairs. A veil of smoke,
drifts down the landing and shifts, ghostlike,
amidst the hallway's shadows. I can smell

her perfume. The smoke holds the dense
aroma of incense burning. Incense always
made me dizzy – its heady fumes hypnotic.
"Death's perfume." I remember an old priest's
cryptic comment when I was an alter boy.
Nuns and priests and devils and holy ghosts
whirl with my intoxication as I stagger to the top.
I grip the banister to keep from swaying.

She stands across the room with her back to me,
dressed in black – a gossamer black with lavish
jet trimmings and lush midnight lace. Her long
raven hair fans like wings across her shoulders
and back. Candles, candelabrums flutter
on bureaus, bed stands. Incense is burning
everywhere. She is singing to herself in a mirror –
some sweet sad street song reminiscent of that long ago
chanteuse they called "the little sparrow" – and applying
red lipstick. Her lost lament sounds like nothing
so much as a lullaby.
I cross myself and stagger in.

TROUBLE TOWN II

Plant closed, her sister up and gone,
nothing but trouble since she got off
the Greyhound. Five days traveling
and everything upside down. Room
by the station, cockroach nation – still,
more than she can afford since she
was expecting free room and board.
At least 'til she got on her feet. Not
that she could ever depend on her sister
or anyone for that matter. She should
have known better, stayed where she
was even though her life was in tatters.
Sheila drinks and wonders what else
can go wrong.
"I'm living in a world of wonder,"
the jukebox plays her favorite song.
"happiness around each corner."
"Buy you a drink?"
She glances in the mirror at the greasy
guy who sits down next to her.
"No thanks. I'm waiting for someone."
She forces a smile, tries not to look
rattled by his zipper scar, demon-
tattooed arms, lightning sideburns.
"Ain't no Prince Charming gonna come,
Hon, not to this dump, if that's who
you're waiting on."
His expression is blank, frank, grim.
"Then I'll learn to live without one."
She shrugs. "So long." She toasts him.

"It's been fun."
"The fun ain't begun."
He studies her and sips his beer.
OK Trouble Town, Sheila sighs, bring
it on. Your day was long but your night
is young.

BETWEEN THE CLOCK AND THE BED

She awakens to the wind's wailing,
through half-closed eyes sees
the dead around her bed.
The rafters creak and the windows rattle.
Snow swirls beyond them in the winter night.
"All dead, all dead."
She shudders, trying to clear her head.
Her head is foggy and her body aches.
She gropes across the room and turns on the light.
Her reflection in the mirror meets her with a shock.
In her dream, she was dancing
in the arms of a young man,
whirling and laughing.

ODE TO RAGDOLL

Your mother was a junkie, your father a drunk.
You dressed in rags and the school kids treated
you like junk. Pretend playmates were all you had.
Life was a ghost's dream way back then.
But things changed. You became a knockout.
Life switched to the fast lane, money and men.
Rags to riches – but it was still pretend.
For love or money? You'd vanish in a blink.
Same old ghost world but now you haunt it in mink.

NIGHT HAWKS

Grey city made of clay,
someday you will melt away.
There was childhood which
ran away, then came living
day to day.
I sit alone in my cheap room,
smoke a cigarette. I read a little,
think. Later I'll go out for a drink.
There will be a woman somewhere –
magical, tragic and mercurial, as
women are.
We'll drink together, sleep together,
talk about nothing in particular
with one another.
The point is to stave off loneliness
for another hour.
Tomorrow I will write a story about
a grey city and a man and a woman
who met in a bar, but their love
was made of clay and it washed away.

STARRY NIGHT

You say:
"No more."
Rise, sigh, turn,
close the door,
take the night away.
Did we ever have it?
Are any of them here to stay?
How did things get this way?
No thunder.
Lightning.
Dramatics.
Just coldness.
A chill that came out
of nowhere to warn us
there can never be a
passionate love affair between us.
You felt it first.
We see a love that cannot last.
Why is a mystery.
We were made for each
other as far as we can
see. Your eyes are sacred and serene
I would try to
fulfill your every dream.
Yet we will never belong
to each other's destiny.

A KISS IS STILL A KISS

I caress the slender neck,
cup my palm around the
voluptuous bottom, breathless,
like a young groom on his
honeymoon, or the star-crossed
lover who magically chances
upon his yearned for other,
eyes closed, heart racing, soul
braced in anticipation of the
coming moment as I tighten
my embrace, press my lips to
the mouth of the bottle, tilt
my head and swallow.

SOLITAIRE

I get to the place,
sit in a corner and wait.
Something is missing,
although everything seems
there – the shadows at the bar
staring in the mirror, the silent
jukebox, TV flickering muted
news in the darkness no one
is watching or trying to hear:
about death and destruction,
Wall Street and war.
And then I see Hope at her table
near the window, huddled over
her cards playing solitaire.
Her charms have tarnished.
Her beauty has vanished. Her
sparkle has faded. The shuffling
cards whisper sadness.

R U B Y

"Love is strong as death,
passion as cruel as the grave."

I read that in a Bible in a cheap hotel.
Got into the habit of looking through them
moving around as I do in my travels with
the band, when we get gigs that is. I play
the guitar, sing some too (I'm a singing fool).
But that's me and Ruby to a tee – love that
strong. And more: it's like coming home
when we're together. We belong to each other.
There are two kinds of love, it says in the Bible,
the soul kind and the bodily kind. We got them
both big time.
Ruby's got her demons though. We all do.
Her mother was a junky and her ole man a drunk.
She ran around in rags and the kids treated her
like junk. Pretend playmates was all she had.
Imaginary boyfriends later on. Life was a ghost's
dream way back when. But things changed.
She became a knockout. Men with money chased
after her – life in the fast lane, living large – she
still can't resist the Diamond Jim charge. For
love or money? Ole Ruby will vanish in a blink.
Same old ghost world, as I see it, 'cept now she
haunts it in mink. But she'll come back, always
does. We were made for each other – got that Good
Book love. I wrote a little song for her. Starts like this:

Hell woman with your flashing eyes
Body heat and lips of fire
Heart from Hades and soul from Hell
Banshee daughter of Beelzebub
Hell woman raging in my brain
Hell woman you're the Devil's dream

BRIEF ENCOUNTER

I met her in a blind alley bar.
She had "Queen of Darkness"
written all over her. Roadkill
dripped from her lips. She drank
from a bottle with a skull and
crossbones on its label. "Are you
the one," she batted her Black Hole
eyes at me, "looking for some fun?"
I downed my beer and went home.

STARCHED NAPKINS

Tea for two on the table,
she stands combing her tangled hair
in the room without a rocking chair.
"I am so glad that you are here."
She says to the full length mirror.
All the doors are locked.
All the clocks have stopped.
But tea will be served with care
in fine China with silverware.

CARNIVAL

Seedy streets, dusty urban corridors –
the carnival, colorful, magical, visiting
our dark corner of the world was always
a treat.
"Your tears fall through rainbows little
one." The gypsy told my girlfriend,
her smile soft and round.
"They are tears of love and happiness.
They form diamonds as the day goes on.
They sparkle in your spirit. One day you
will cash them in. You know love's
butterflies keep us alive.
Keys made of moonlight open doors at
Midnight."
Cheap fun, the carnie crown with its clowns.
They helped us get though the recession.
I hope they still come around.

OUR LOVE

A whisper in a shadow.
A slow dance in the moon's
glow. Our silhouettes on a
white wall, like a cinematic
shot captured in our love's
flow.

NOCTURNE

There's a nightclub in a cellar (in my dream)
small, dark, empty. A ghost woman in a
gossamer gown sits at a piano under a spotlight.
She sings:

man in the moon
lord of the night
talk to the whispering
winds in their flight
man in the moon
tell them to sigh
I have a new love

The singer's eyes are like holy mysteries.
Her pale skin is so perfect, it seems painted on.
Her voice is like something you'd hear in heaven, and
I'm wondering if she sings her love song to everyone,
lying on a slab in the county morgue.

SWEET DREAMS ARE MADE OF THIS

drifter digs
you open the door and flop into bed
a single naked light bulb hangs from a ceiling chain
devil shapes toss the room, as its harsh light swings
with the window's wind

each night I hear the exiles doing pratfalls in the dark
they stagger back and forth to the washroom down the hall
or try to maneuver through their tiny flops

across the alley a back street lounge sleep streams until dawn
jazz and blues fill the night with saxophones and wailing songs
silhouettes slow dance in the windows

I watch them through my window, pillow propped against a wall
sipping rye and blowing smoke while the demons shift around

the music wraps the night in dream
I hold you in a memory

PERFECT STORM

Rain, just the same – you as
sunlight shining in Smokey's bar,
yellow slicker, golden hair.
You could come over to me.
We could drink, discuss how
not to make the same mistakes,
discuss life's gives and takes.
I could go over to you. But I can't –
because I remember those black
mascara smears running down
your face with your tears.

THE ORCHARD

An ice-white sky with silvery
light shivering through the
swirling snow, as we bundle
through the cold. The raw
winds blow. Frozen to the
bone, we struggle home, across
downy drifts of death, both of us
draped in shrouds of mystic
whiteness, our old car abandoned
by the side of the road. "I'm
getting old." Hester chatters and
grabs my hand as we stumble together
through the spectral land. There's
still a ways to go. Both of us
know that the ground, somewhere
below, is all too ready and willing
to claim us as its own. But we've
been here, done this, and we'll
do it again, because we're never
leaving this godforsaken land —
not as long as our orchard blossoms
in its season.

REX SEXTON

ARCHIVAL

As in a dark cave,
lips pressed together,
spellbound as sleepwalkers,
hearts beating faster,
rain pounding down,
arms holding each other,
bodies merging together,
"You Send Me" now a
memory playing that night
long ago on an old car radio.

STORMY NIGHT

It's still raining. I bundle
into the bistro and sit down
across from her at the candlelit
table, hoping I don't look too
disheveled. I drop my book
bag on the floor and toe it
under cover as if it contained
anything important.
"No rain no rainbow?" I offer.
Our table is in a corner by the
window. Shapeless figures shuffle
to and fro, hidden under umbrellas,
like plodding turtles. She sighs and
studies the menu as if we were going
to order anything except the cheapest
items presented on the menu. The
nightly crowd slowly gathers, there
is violin music, whispers and laughter.
"Beyond the world's tears there are
stars?" I wonder.
She smiles. "The night is ours."

237

AGAIN

Years like dried leaves
blowing in the winter wind.
Your breathing next to mine
again, your body next to mine
again, your heart beating next
to mine again – I see your eyes
in heaven, hear your laughter
in the wind. In every dream
you are near me. I can never
love again.

BURIED TREASURES

Bring me vast riches – not little things
like diamond rings, or fame or wealth
or kingdom's keys, power, glory.
Who needs such things? Bring me
memories of jubilees, love and joy
and families. You know where to
find them. Tucked away in treasure
chests where those who shared them
went to rest.

THE MAGICIAN

Softly in the dark,
the Magician slips
past the bolted locks,
up the slender, spiral staircase.
down the narrow, dimly-lit hallway,
though the silent, moonlit bedchambers,
out the window and over the roof –
as quiet as a shadow,
draped in his midnight magic black cloak,
carrying his satchel of starlight and moonglow,
as he dusts the night with dream.

THE KISS GOODNIGHT

Somber in the soft dusk
with sleep coming on
I think about the best
way to lay life's wonders
down. Of course, somehow
with a smile on my face. No
sour grapes. Death is everyone's
fate.
I must lay my long mirror down.
The future belongs to those who
are coming. I'll greet them as I
can, leave them a little something.
Grace and beauty has its way.

"THE STUDIO"

Back and forth, left to right, like a moth around a candle, like a bat in flight. Hand and eye mesmerized, watching the slash of blazing colors crisscross, collide, slowly erasing any trace of the screaming face that stares at me starkly from each blank canvas like a maniac unleashed, until it is magically replaced by occult incantations and voodoo rites, which people take for art – line, form, hues, shapes, all rainbows in a dream of amazing grace.

It is cold in the studio, dead of winter in the windows, sky a shroud, yet fever bright from incandescent light. I shiver and inhale another coffin nail. On the canvas, faceless strangers come and go, as shadows sweep across a land, where mists envelop each pale ghost lost in a nimbus about to disappear like smoke.

As I was made to vanish everyday long ago when I began this mystic, art making ritual at the school of The Immaculate Conception Cathedral in Chicago, where the nuns would banish me, perfunctorily, from the classroom to the coat closet, where I was supposed to sit in the dark and repent for drawing in my notebook instead of pondering my textbook and failing to pay attention to whatever they were saying about math, history, geography, religion.

The ragman's horse drawn wagon ... the vendors and the junkman ... the blind man tending his news stand ... the derelicts picking through trash cans ... the knife-sharpener bent over his whetstone, sparks flying in every direction ... the pushcarts clattering through potholes ... the pigeon lady tossing her bread crumbs ... the organ grinder's uniformed monkey tipping his cap to everyone for money ... the storefronts' food displays, gathering flies under the awnings' shade ... the maze of narrow, ramshackle, streets crowded with houses, tenements, factories ... the pig trucks, cattle trucks, poultry trucks, crisscrossing from every direction (chased by the mutts who add to the bedlam) ... the nuns sweeping down the parish steps, winds rippling their holy black habits ... the priests in their robes and vestments praying in candlelight and incense ... the old women in babushkas telling their rosaries in sanctified stillness ... the legions of raggedy kids swarming the walks and streets and parks (amidst a menagerie of birds and cats and squirrels) – I drew everything in the neighborhood, plus devils, angels, circus clowns, spaceships, clipper ships, dinosaurs, and my daily banishment to solitary only contributed to my delinquency. In the dark and silent closet I would lay on my stomach, where the light filtered through the crack beneath the door and draw more.

NIGHT RIDE

I steal a ride with the ragman,
around us raw winds rip.
He lashes his horse down the foggy streets,
wagon wheels rattling like demons in the mist.
Ghost garments fly through the air,
land in his cart on angel wings –
wedding gowns yellowed with age,
threadbare suits, faded pants and shirts,
overcoats, baby bonnets, babushkas,
feathered hats and lingerie.

The howling winds form a chorus,
singing songs as we chase through the streets
of joy and sorrow, birth and death – phantom
voices in a holy dream.

Clothes swoop down like spirits.
Scraps of lives float everywhere.

ETERNITIES COLLIDE

I nod my head one more time.
Life is gone.
Why would it last?
But not so fast.
I saw the universe shoot past,
stars and moons and meteors,
comets, planets.
I wonder if in my new nakedness
I will be reborn again into another
mess like the one I just left?
Will I have to do it all over again,
world without end, through some
construct of reincarnation?
Will this mortal toil never end?
Shadows fly past me in little
cocoons, dead souls traveling in
their worn out carcasses into
something new: flowers, birds,
monkeys, bees, maybe humans
again? Will the sun never set?
Isn't the cosmos done with me yet?
Why not, instead of all this rebirth,
life after death, whatever you want
to call it, that singular satisfying
of peace calming the tumult down.

IN DREAM

Lost in the moon's glow
We chased the dream shadows
Down the lanes of love's wonder
Through of heart's mysteries
Holding each other
We waltzed round a rainbow
Dancing on stardust
To our own melody

Goodbye my darling
It's been good to know you
Farewell my angel
Your love swept me away
So long my lady
May sweet dreams enfold you
We'll walk again in the moon's glow someday

Through the glass darkly
The moon casts your shadow
In dreams I pursue you
Through the soft veils of sleep
I see your smile in the sunrise
With the first glow of morning
I hear your voice on the wind
I feel you with me when twilight descends

Farewell my lovely
It's been good to know you
Goodbye my darling
Our love will never fade

So long my lady
May sweet dreams enfold you
We'll dance together
On the stardust again

CITY OF WIND

We blew up chicken gullets, like balloons,
for the girls to carry around on strings
and played pirate with sharpened stockyard bones
which we sheathed in our clothesline belts, like swords,
marauding through the neighborhood

Along the sidewalks, the girls played hopscotch,
arms raised in the air like wings,
hopping toward the Blue Sky
with tiny, one-footed leaps.

Angels flew in the city of wind,
around the steeples of the churches,
over the rooftops of the tenements,
under the viaducts and bridges,
through the gangways of the houses
down the narrow streets and alleys,
above the fuming slaughterhouse chimneys
billowing black smoke into the wind.

EPILOGUE

"DODGING BULLETS"

He couldn't leave bad enough alone, Conti's doctor, he had to make it worse.

"You're a walking dead man."

He said to Conti after his exam.

"Excuse me?"

"Can I make it plainer? Your days are numbered. You smoke like a chimney, drink like a fish, eat uppers and downers out of a candy dish. How many years have I been warning you about that?"

"I'm an artist!" Conti laughed.

"OK artist you want to know what's wrong with this picture? Even after treatment you won't last a year."

Top flight physician, Conti's sawbones, he had to admit. Beside manner? Conti wasn't sure about that.

* * *

"A cat has nine lives." Conte's wife said when she too learned he had cancer of the lungs. "So, do you. You'll come through."

True, Conti thought as he watched his wife stir the soup which simmered on the stove.

He had had his bouts with death. The first one right off the bat, having rheumatic fever plus pneumonia when he was four. Death came early, knocking at his door. Conti knew death and he wondered if he had ultimately learned anything from it that he had passed on to illuminate living one's life? Death and dying had become part of Conti's painting

251

and writing far more than he ever wanted. So much so Conti felt like he was haunted.

Every day, as kids, they watched the trucks haul cattle and pigs to the slaughter houses in his neighborhood. The trucks were rolling wooden cages. The cows and pigs looked pathetic.

You could hear them moan and screech all the way down the block.

Their fathers worked in the yards as butchers or sausage makers. Even as Mallet men, the guys that crushed skulls with spiked sledge hammers for a living. Their fathers drank a lot after work. Who could blame them? One day they would work there, too, they knew. They'd need a drink as well.

Blood and guts, slaughtered flesh, maybe all that death got Conti thinking about the meaning of life. Life looked pretty scary, grim and grisly. He thought a lot about art, too.

Maybe the act of creation was a counter to all the destruction? As a kid, he was dazzled by the stained glass windows in the neighborhood Cathedral. He tried to imitate them with cheap watercolor pictures. He liked to listen to the biblical stories as well: Noah's Ark, David and Goliath, Moses, Jesus. Conti was equally dazzled by the comic strips. He used to create his own – stories, captions, pictures, heroes and villains, often while his grammar school classes were going on, which got him in a lot of trouble with the nuns. He always knew what he was going to do with his life, paint and write. That was the unstated plan. Come hell or high water if need be to the bitter end.

A tough row to hoe it turned out. Conti lived in many ghettos and slums, waiting for his art to catch on, stories too. He went cold and hungry many a day. Slum death, he saw a lot of that, overdoses, shootings, stabbings. Somehow he survived them.

Hard times in tough places. Conti found himself thinking, as the soup bubbled in its kettle, about what his doctor said: "walking dead." Dead-end kid, rebel without a cause, with one ultimately: poet, activist, artist, creating works that were socially conscious, that challenged injustice,

Conti spent a lifetime with the have-nots. One critic called him "a voice for the powerless." They were a doomed lot. One generation after the next, from birth to death, kept down by the odds that are against them from day one – poverty, racism, discrimination, poor educations.

Eyes downcast, because there's nothing to look forward to, voices just mumbles, ghostly voices like perpetual penitents fearful of a wrathful God – not the biblical God but the God of American Capitalism which ruled them with policemen, boss men, crooked politicians, those were his neighbors, friends. There is no free will in the ghetto. (No free will anywhere if you want to get technical.) Free will really means having options (that illusion of choosing things). Options are bought and sold, they are purchased from actual or existential gifts of silver or gold.

Conti was born with a silver tongue (not spoon) in his mouth. Besides his ability to think lucidly and speak effectively, he had other marketable blessings. (Not the God kind, the atoms and ifs kind which are all you're going to find.) He was born white. Even more then, way back when, it would trump anything a person of color had to offer, every time. Conti eventually became foreman or manager of any hardscrabble job for which he hired on. He never stayed long, not until he wanted to get serious about a pension. And manager was his limit. He needed to master his wild and crazy artwork. Even that paid off in the end.

As a poet and activist, Conti sought a world in which all those who are blessed help the rest. Was that too much to ask?

* * *

Guns and slums, a lifetime of danger and there he was, lying and dying in his bed. Did he still have time to do some good? Conti wondered. Had he done anything in his life for which he could be proud? Was that what life was about, being content with yourself? Passing something on to future generations like knowledge, wisdom, legacies from fortunes? Or was it a meaningless thing, pointless and self-serving? How did death and dying play into that? Do you grab it all while you can or out of empathy pass some on to the less fortunate of your fellow man?

Conti had survived a lot more than Rachael could ever guess, especially if you counted the bullets he dodged in his gangbanging youth when he was shot at by cops, rival gangs, and once was almost blown up in a restaurant when the Greek mob in his neighborhood tried to blow up the Italian hoods. What fools. Factor in the uppers, downers, caffeine, tobacco Conti habitually consumed and as far as cashing it in goes, Conti was long overdue. What a mess. More slaughter house stuff, only with his fellow man not animals. And then there was that war which he never asked for, the draft, the protests.

Candles and shadows, whispers and echoes, windows and mirrors, lit by the moon's glow; Conti thought as he began to drift off, and on the card table, the hand that life dealt you. Win or lose, living's a gamble. If you came from where he did, the odds were against you.

If you didn't like the odds, go find a rainbow. They say we have souls. Is that what the body knows? They say life's a dream. Ever hear someone scream?

Should he scream? Conti wondered.

Like a dark crime Time slowly kills the body and the mind. Last year a stroke, before that kidney cancer, ten years ago, hanging an art show, he scrambled his brains when he fell off a ladder. The doctors gave him no chance whatsoever. On top of the busted skull he had another interesting dilemma to them, about which they decided to lecture. He was in a waking coma. His brain was asleep but his mind functioned as normal.

"This is Mr. Conti." The M.D.s would introduce him to each class they brought into his room. "He's dying and there's nothing we can do for him. Medically, although his eyes are open, and he speaks quite lucidly, he's fast asleep in a coma. If you have any questions feel free to ask him."

Conti had had a "sleeping" coma when he was eighteen. Maybe that's why he was able to fight this one? He flatlined then, died in a Chicago hospital and, some would say, went to heaven. It was one of those tunnel and light experiences, extremely vivid. He never figured out what happened. He expired and traveled to another dimension?

Like a bullet from the barrel of a gun he shot into a blaze of light as brilliant as the sun. Light so bright … light everywhere … a golden, glistening radiance that went on forever. "What the hell is this?" Conti wondered, as he pondered the splendor. God? Heaven? The luminescence not only enveloped him it coursed through his being like nuclear explosions. His phantom body roiled in ecstasy, cell by cell, each atom an individual exhilaration, while his mind was a crystalline prism sparkling with serenity and wisdom. Too late to get religion but he didn't seem to need one. He was floating in Nirvana? The hereafter? Another dimension? "Energy is eternal delight." Conti recalled a line by William Blake who had written often about his travels in another dimension. Spinal meningitis, from maddening pain, raging fever to Nirvana. This wasn't a coma or a dream in a delirium. He knew those well. He had done that, been there. This was nothing anyone could imagine, nothing anyone could fathom. "I am alive and I am real!" The puppet, Pinocchio, exclaimed when he was turned by magic into a human being. Conti had that same feeling. The life he had lived before this moment was zero by comparison. It was some kind of murky, shadow existence.

Life after life? Or a trick of the dying mind? He studied physics in college when he was stationed at the Pentagon. It was possible that there were other dimensions. Maybe leaving the body was how you reached them? Conti put the experience in his last book. Afterlife sells, at least, better than anything else he'd written. Two years later he was still getting calls for radio interviews. People need hope. Is there? Who knows. If his wife was right, maybe Conti was in for a sequel?

255

All he could do was stay tuned. With that last thought it was time for dreamland.

* * *

"Cries from the clinic:" Conti stared at the ceiling, "I count sheep but can't sleep." Ha! He would be up all night, again, staring at the nightlight above his hospital bed. As usual the meds were defective, at least on him. Six days, seven nights of insomnia and that damned tiny glow through which his mind reeled in hypnotic turmoil, conjuring up chaotic images of disaster and horror and bedlam and bloody murder – Technicolor hallucinations Conti couldn't stop or control. Conti had rushed to ER with a hundred and three fever. Pneumonia again, a side effect of the massive doses of chemotherapy and radiation he was given each day to try to arrest and kill the cancer in his lungs. Too many cigarettes, a necessary antidote to writer's block. You puff and puff until something comes up. But maybe it wasn't cigarettes. Maybe it was asbestos, he'd been around it enough, working in factories, living in tenements.

All Conti's sheep were black, until the demon looking down from the ceiling blew them up. Then they were red and dead – the chemo and radiation probably put that stuff in his perpetually foggy head. Conti started thinking about the pleasure of smoking, of drinking, the pleasure of sex. Not much of these lately, only on his best days. The treatments kicked his ass.

If he hadn't been receiving these God-awful treatments which caused nausea, vomiting, diarrhea, dizziness, headaches, abdominal pain, gastrointestinal calamities, burning, chocking, he would have been dead shortly after he started coughing up blood from the tumor. His cancer was fierce and aggressive. The treatments were no cure. They just kept death from the door, momentarily. Now he was coughing up phlegm from pneumonia. The chemo eradicates the immune system.

It also weakens the bones. His ribs were cracked from gagging on his mucus.

Extremely painful, they would have to try to fix that soon. They did that by more radiation but he would have to live with the broken ribs until his chemo was completely done, another month at the very least. Perhaps two.

"My book." Conti forced himself to think about something else. His book was getting good reviews. But they all had. Of course, he was glad. But the name of the game was advertising. The little company in Boston that published him couldn't afford to toss the millions around that was needed these days to get a book on and off the shelves. No one in America read much. Not much of anything challenging anyway. It was different elsewhere – Europe, Asia, Canada, the Eastern Block, Conti's friends in Russia. American men weren't even on the book marketing radar screen. Three quarters of the books published, here, were by and for women.

The one quarter written by men, here, were aimed at the woman audience. What did Hemmingway say about reading books and real men. If you didn't you weren't one? Sometimes there were deep efforts by elite writers published by university presses.

These were few and far between – too cost prohibitive.

It was all about money. "50 Shades of Gray." Printing junk for the lowest common denominator. A full-page ad in the New York Times cost one hundred thousand dollars a pop and then there's LA, Chicago, Houston etc. No one knew his books were out there. He couldn't afford to tell them. They wouldn't want them anyway. Crime, sex, romance, melodrama – rarely anything you can sink your teeth into. That's what was featured each week in the New York Times. Painting was a different story. There was a sophisticated market interested in complex creations, at least visual ones. In that endeavor, Conti made money.

Was there any moral to this story? At night, on the town, when the exotics abound, their presence so rarefied they threaten to disappear before our eyes, the wealthy and cultured, exquisite in thought and appearance, decorate the night with their radiant existence.

There are the others as splendid who offer deliverance from the inevitability of the oncoming entropy, where all things stop and cease to be. They carry the spirit lamps that light dark corners – poets, artists, midnight lovers. They help illuminate the heavens, although they rarely inhabit them. That honor is for the pure of soul, the generous of spirit, of thought and goal. The monosyllabic public (the rest) has the earth to grunt and bark upon till kingdom come.

They are everywhere, everywhere trying to find a simple statement they can understand. That's a lot for them.

Conti's lyrical novella would rot on the vine, like an exotic fruit on an uninhabited island.

Like he was rotting in his skin! Jesus, that demon nightlight beam again! It's not like he was going to devote a novel to this like Solzhenitsyn. The treatments were almost done. Give him a little time and he'd be back on the scene, exhibiting paintings, giving poetry readings. Maybe not for as long as he thought before he was hit by this bomb. But that was some else's sad song.

* * *

Black coat, hat, suit, shoes, hair, you stand there. Conti mused. There is no shelter from your cold stare. Like puppets we dangle from the strings of the master. If we don't lurch about we'll knock nothing over.

Sleepwalkers, we engage our brains, use our limbs. I act, therefore I am. Conti went on remembering his science lessons. So do atoms. Action, reaction, cause, effect, from birth to death, through hell and back, even the blood runs black, like death through our veins.

Like you my grim friend. Conti sighed.

Being and Nothingness were all the same. Unfurl your fingers, unclench your hand, reach for your dream through the candle's flame.

I might as well keep walking, Conti lay awake in the cancer ward thinking, just keep walking until I find the way. Clouds tangle in the restless sky. A pale moon shines. In this darkness one feels a presence. Some say that it is heaven sent, others that it is only a random moment – that phantom space between world and time where reality and illusion intertwine and Genesis becomes a nursery rhyme. Living, dying, what did it mean?

Life is a strange place to stay. Conti smiled. Misfits meet and play, lost souls gather and pray, longing haunts each day.

Eternal life? Conti puzzled. Just one and you're done? Did Conti even care at this point? He would find out soon. What had life been anyway? A dream? That's what it seemed.

Most dreams are out of your reach. But you dream them anyway, even though they leave you more lost and miserable, amidst the rubble of your troubles, than if you had let them go, knowing they were a no show.

Life is a stormy road. Conti reflected. You head for a dead end as soon as you begin.

Somewhere in the middle you start to understand that you are a stranger in a no man's land where no one speaks your language and no one understands. It is the same for everyone. Yet passion burns and souls yearn and while dreams die they live again.

There was lots of whiskey for Conti in his life, warm friends, loving women, starry-eyed children eager to begin. He'd love to do it again.

" S K E L E T O N   K E Y "
(Unfinished)

Lucky − Cody leaned into the light, took a drag off his cigarette and studied the letter. Had it arrived a day later, it could have spent a month in the mail room at the Boston Center for the Arts, waiting for him to return from Chicago.

> Dear Mr. Cody:
>
> Congratulations! This letter is to inform you that you are the recipient of the 1982 Jason C. Tucker Award for Best New Chapbook.
>
> Your chapbook entitled, "Dark Clouds" has been selected for this award from 2,000 entries.
>
> The Chapbook will be published by Ringquest and Locks and will be available in six months. A check for $500 is enclosed.
>
> Thank you for your entry and our best wishes on your great accomplishment.
>
> Sincerely,
> Ronald Young
> Editor-in-Chief
> The Briar Canyon Review

This was big news for Cody. He was thirty-two years old and this was his first writing award. "Lucky," Cody sighed. He may be able to use this as an acknowledgement to make something more of his life than starving artist and writer. He had just gotten an Associate Degree in painting on the G. I. Bill. He wanted to move to New York, where all of the publishers were and try to establish a life in the writing world. Either world, actually, but, maybe, he could get a job as a Reader or Junior Editor for some New York agent or publisher. If not that, then as soon he completed his degree, he could try to teach somewhere. But, he had to get to New York. He was a novelist, or wanted to be one more than anything. He wanted to write stories about people's lives. Right now, he was writing about the sad lives in ghettos. Cody had spent most of his life in them. Right now, in Boston, as a poor artist, in a slum. Boston had nothing left to offer him.

The line moved along, up the platform to the tracks. Cody finished his cigarette. He read the poem from his book "Dark Clouds."

> They gather in the ghettos
> like preachers frozen in spirit.
> Another black son has been killed
> by a white policeman for no
> apparent reason.
> Massive arms flail as the
> sorrowful brethren try to
> console the younger congregation,
> still a realm of graves filled
> with the skeletons of slaves.
> If only their lives could be
> set free.
> If only they could release the chains
> That bind them to hatred, injustice
> and bigotry.

Cody swallowed hard. He searched the book for his favorite poem, recently written, which described best his many years in Boston.

CAPE NIGHTS

Our turbulent flights from the ghettos
of Boston where we lived amidst the
damned as starving artists in a no-man's-
land.
We'd camp on the beach in my rusted
VW Van. The old junker had traveled
the world. It was a gift from an and elderly
art patron, a kind and thoughtful man.
Every now and then he would buy one of my
paintings from the Boston Center For The Arts.
I hear he lived in a mansion.
The van came in handy.
I'd transport the works from the Center sculptors'
for a small fee.
I'd use this money to pay for our
trips to the Cape. Six of us, three
couples, would make the journey north.
None of us owned anything. We probably never would.
We'd make love in the sand, danceon the crashing waves.
We saw freedom in the ocean. Freedom in
the infinite possibilities of our visions.
Our heads were filled with great dreams
we knew we'd never wake from.

Cody tucked the chapbook into his duffle bag and put the bag in
the overhead rack. His heart pounded. He felt light-headed from the
unexpected news. He would write to the editor when he reached Chicago.
Tomorrow his father would pick him up and he would spend the next
day with his parents. The following day, his father would take him to

the VA hospital for the operation. After that, Cody had to get together with his brother about a job. Cody needed money to make his New York move. His brother had a booming business – renovating houses. Cody would hang in and stay in Chicago. For as long as it took to put a stake together.

Cody's kind of town, Chicago?

Back of the factories sprawled a blue-collar badlands which often proved deadly.

Train yards loaded with freight cars, a maze of narrow crisscrossing streets cluttered with small shops, plants and factories, pubs, bars, seedy lounges all embedded amidst humble, rickety, dilapidated dwellings, turned this tract of urban blight into a brawling, hard-drinking challenge for any night. Big Red, Tall Paul, Slim Jim, Fat Pete, The Brago Brothers, the Dempsy Brothers, it was fight or flight everywhere you looked, every step you took. How did he fair? He didn't make it out of there without a police record – grand theft auto, burglary, dealing, shoplifting, assault and battery. It came with the trouble town territory. It could have been worse. He could have bought it from a bullet early on, like many of his friends.

They were surrounded by Chicago. The Chi-town gangs would come at them from every direction. They fought them to a standstill, measure for measure, over drugs, hock shops to handle stolen goods, competitive heists OK'd by gangsters for a cut. The gangs were ready for anything. They'd take them on, never back down. He graduated from the school of hard knocks, which informed his vision of empathy for those whom fate dealt a bad hand.

"So you lived in New York?" Cody's brother asked the next day.

"No. I stayed there three months just to see how much it costs. I'll need a big stake to move there, at least three grand. I'll have to get settled, find a job that works."

Bob was impressed by Cody's poetry award of five hundred dollars. Everyone was impressed. His parents were flabbergasted. They had a great dinner together and celebrated. Now he and his brother were drinking beers and trying to figure things out.

"I have a full crew." Bob lit a cigarette. "They're all good. I expect them all to stay the season. The money is rolling in. I only need an extra or two for emergency use. That's two hundred a week. I also have a friend, who runs a small restaurant. It's mainly a lunch place. He needs a manager. That should give you a couple more hundred plus bartending tips. You can flop at my house. It's the center for everything. You can eat there, too. The freezer is always full."

Cody was tall and gaunt. In high school his sports were track and basketball. His little brother however was a giant. He played football in school and wrestled. Running a construction crew was right up his alley. He reached out to find new ways in the old days.

Bob Cody was responsible for the upkeep of a thousand unit apartment complex, painting, dry wall, etc., as needs came up. He had a crew of about a dozen. Some were Mexican immigrants carrying green cards. A handful of others were experts at mansion renovation. Right now, he was bringing it in hand over fist, but the Carter administration was spiraling down and interest rates were shooting through the roof. He was afraid he was going to lose business.

"We'll set records this year so you should be just fine. Next year's a different story. The economy will crash. Nothing for you to worry about. Give my regards to Broadway," he lifted his glass and smiled.

As far as the restaurant went, it was an old family place for him. It one time it was a ____ alley. ____ were possibilities there. The Mayor of the town would for laughs

265

II

"Oranges and lemons,
Say the bells of St. Clement's.

You owe me five farthings,
Say the bells of St. Martin's.

When will you pay me?
Say the bells of Old Bailey.

When I grow rich,
Say the bells of Shoreditch.

When will that be?
Say the bells of Stepney.

I do not know,
Says the great bell of Bow.

Here comes a candle to light you to bed,
And here comes a chopper to chop off your head!"

The cooked books of the Pisano Restaurant reminded Cody of that classic nursery rhyme about the churches of England talking finances together. Pete Pesche had been casually and thoughtlessly using a local Veterans Administration to bolster up his family restaurant. Pete was in charge of the whole Veterans Administration for the town. The job came with powerful political influence. The salary he got was enormous. He was in charge of fish fries, weddings, parties, elections. In the midst of this dynasty he controlled, he remained a really nice restaurant man. However, he wasn't paying attention to the trouble he was in. Basically, he was embezzling. Twenty thousand dollars so far had gone into his own private business. This was a federal offense. The FBI could easily get in on it. Pete would be out on the street then left in prison. There were no shades of grey with this as far as Cody could see. It was all black and white.

Cody was born blonde. They called him "Whitey" all through grammar school. In high school, however, his hair dramatically transformed into sliver grey. Cody wore it short and had a military look. This is a good look to wear throughout life. People take you more seriously. Of course, that wasn't true in the art world. When Cody enrolled at the art center straight from the army, the artists nicknamed him Captain America. Cody had to hand out some knuckle sandwiches to stop that banter. Cody also, like many visual artists, had piercing eyes, blue in his case. Between the hair and the eyes, his appearance was quite striking.

Now, at the restaurant, on the phone all morning with Pete Pesche, the chemistry wasn't working. Pesche fired him right off. Cody wasn't putting up with that guff. He called him back and threatened him with calling the Feds, himself.

"Mama Mia!" Cody rubbed his forehead. The smartest thing for Cody to have done would be to fix up the restaurant as best he could, borrow a few grand from the VA and head for New York. Instead, he decided to be honest and turn everything upside down.

The problem with Pisano's was that everyone for twenty years from Pete to his brother to his daughter, the cook Paulo and even the old man, who worked the late bar, had been robbing the place blind. Everyone had been grabbing a few bucks here and there.

His daughter Cindy just had a baby. She wanted to sit home with her kid, not work here. Tony, Pete's son-in-law, just got a job – courtesy of Pete – with the sheriff's department. He was done with this, too. Paulo, the cook, was the victor here. Cody didn't know if Pete could use him at the VA, but he was going to help him out by giving up his money for selling the joint so he could get a new start.

This was a total bust for Cody. Maybe, his brother could find some more work for him beyond the season? He would have to stay in Chicago to put some savings together.

Cody made some more notes about the restaurant's workings and went back into the bar. Cindy had been taking care of his bartendering while he talked with her father. Cody had told them all of his plans to sell the place. They all thought this wouldn't happen, but they didn't know the whole story.

The bar sat twenty. It was half full, the side tables were also more than half filled. It was a clean, bright, cheerful, lunch of soup and sandwiches and generous drinks. Paulo was a good cook, a standup guy. You couldn't fault him for stealing from the cookie jar to give his family a better life. Now they would be out in the street. Cody felt bad about it.

"I'm the new bartender, Cody."

Cody stopped to talk to a few WWII veterans. "I'm going to buy the next round." He began pouring drinks from the bar.

His brother just called. He needed a one bedroom apartment painted by morning. Cody figured four hours for the small job. His brother paid fifty dollars for one bedroom, one hundred for two. His brother paid good wages. He would work on it tonight, after he closed Pisano's.

He would call the late night bartender, whose shift was five till ten, and have him come to work an hour early. He could do the job in four hours. On the way to the apartment complex, Cody cashed his prize check. He had no clue knew where more was going to come from. He figured that would be his expense money for a while.

> Night haunts, night spirits,
> slipping through moonlit rooms,
> down starlit stairways,
> past mystery doorways into dream chambers,
> where love potions splash on ice,
> and music plays magic melodies

for sleep walkers who dance in a trance,
arms holding each other,
eyes blazing with rapture,
mouths pressed together,
as they devour each other,
before youth is over.

Cody had become enchanted by the night life scene on the Gold Coast of Chicago. It rivaled anything he had seen in Paris or New York. Chicago had a population of three million. It was a giant world class city with a huge art scene, exclusive stores, shops, galleries and expensive car dealers.

"Confined in my cloud prison,
I watch a rainbow arch across the heavens.
Dreams shimmer through fate's prism.
I fall through life's crystal ball."

269

Made in the USA
Middletown, DE
11 May 2017